Contents

Photographs and illustrations copyright: Jennifer Laing or Lloyd Laing
(See also acknowledgments)

Editor
Greg Payne

Design Editor
Liz Wright

Origination
Sally Robinson

Published by
Greenlight Publishing
The Publishing House, 119 Newland Street
Witham, Essex CM8 1WF
Tel: 01376 521900 **Fax:** 01376 521901
mail@greenlightpublishing.co.uk
www.greenlightpublishing.co.uk

Printed in Great Britain

ISBN 1 897738 20X
© 2004 Greenlight Publishing

The Author

Jennifer Laing was taken to her first "bumpy" field at the age of four and retains clear memories of investigating the mouldering hassocks in the derelict church of the deserted medieval village. After further adventures in both past and present she discovered the "Decipherment of Linear B" by Michael Ventris that, quirkily, inspired her to read Ancient and Medieval History and Archaeology at university.

Eschewing careers in insurance or as a nanny (the only posts she remembers being offered) on the grounds they were mostly indoors she worked on excavations fulltime for nearly two years. Realising that the indoor life had a lot to commend it, and finding that her first attempt to gain a book contract was immediately successful she began freelance lecturing and writing on history and archaeology from 1973 to 1987. After three years on a university research fellowship, a domestic relocation in 1990 necessitated her returning to the reclusive occupation of writing about the past. This was enlivened by the occasional unpaid fieldwork with Lloyd Laing (an academic archaeologist who was given his first Roman coin at the age of 10) with whom she has sometimes collaborated as a writer.

Acknowledgements

The photographs used in Figs.33 and 34 were by Ed Archer, Figs.57 and 58 by Andrew Poulter, Figs.63 and 64 by Bob Howard, Fig.67 by Amy Bogaard and Fig.68 by Robert Craigie. Thanks to them for allowing me to use their pictures, to Neil Faulkner and his team at Sedgeford, the Greenlight team and Lloyd, for help in making this book possible.

Introduction

This work aims to answer some of the many questions people ask archaeologists. Although there is a mass of books, TV programmes and practical events dealing with archaeology, these are inevitably related to specific topics. The very width of the subject can leave some mystifying gaps in knowledge.

I have drawn together all the basic questions that I have been asked over the years. These have come from a very wide cross section of the population including academics and other professionals, school children, friends and evening class members. I have written the book in a form that can be dipped into for reference rather than necessarily read in its entirety. The aim is that the reader should be able to add to his/her existing knowledge without needing to wade through already well-understood material.

This book is not intended to be an "encyclopaedia" but rather to give a flavour of what there is to know. A list of further reading, which incorporates most of my sources, is appended. In general I have used examples from Britain.

The most common question I have been asked has been "How do you know it is Roman?" (Or medieval, Dark Age etc). The question is often impossible to answer adequately on a muddy site in the rain, when everyone is longing for a nice cup of tea.

Occasionally, perhaps to counter the jargon, members of the public wrap up perfectly reasonable questions under facetiousness. My favourite was, "Why were the Romans 6in tall?" This was a reference to why the site in question had been reduced to foundations. Whichever way the question is asked, the interrogator usually wants reassurance that archaeologists are not simply making it all up.

Archaeologists use a strange mixture of the technical ("The destruction level is datable to after the third quarter of the 1st century AD but does not post-date the later Hadrianic period."); the practical ("There is 1.3 metres of stratigraphy."); the baffling ("It's a robber trench.") and the colloquial ("There's a lot of archaeology down there."). The latter is irritatingly ungrammatical shorthand for the phrase "archaeologically significant remains".

The answers to such questions lie in the complex interaction of different approaches and methods - from the painstaking collection of data to the application of logic and deduction in order to make interpretations. The study has built up over several centuries, incorporating the theoretical and the practical, and from the start had an uneasy relationship with illicit looting and wanton destruction.

One rule of thumb I have found useful is that if the answers make little or no sense, it is worth considering that the questions themselves are "wrong" (ie it is always worth closely scrutinising any underlying assumptions). This can be difficult if scholars come from different disciplines with different approaches. Archaeology (which like most other subjects prides itself in being a dispassionate study) does excite very strong emotions and many controversies are fuelled by it - possibly because it has traditionally been associated with items of great financial value.

When I was a student, reading Ancient and Medieval History and Archaeology, the tensions between the subjects were apparent in the phrase, constantly quoted by historians, that "archaeology is merely the handmaid of history". More recently, it has appeared to become merely the "hobby of science". Yet, when specialists from different disciplines collaborate, spectacular results are often achieved. Fortunately, to judge by the increasing media coverage of such events, it appears that this is the route ahead.

Vellum page from a "Book of Hours", Paris, 15th century.

8

Chapter 1

What is Archaeology?

Archaeology is the study of the human past from its material remains, and therefore can make use of every conceivable subject in both arts and sciences. This factor gives it wide appeal and allows everyone to be involved. However, it also inevitably means that nobody can "know it all". Much confusion seems to arise over archaeology's relationship to history which, although also a wide-ranging study of the past, is (for periods prior to the 20th century) primarily concerned with the written word. History forms the basic framework of study since the past is divided into prehistoric (before history) and historic periods.

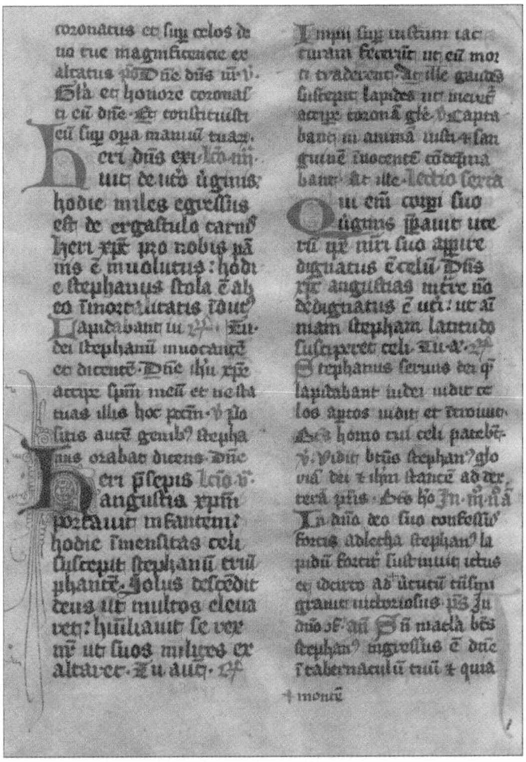

When did history begin?

Historical dates are provided by documentary sources, which (obviously) presuppose the use of writing. However, not all writing can be proven to represent words or sentences and not all societies with writing used it to record events - sometimes it was used for magical purposes.

Writing has been found on many different materials - papyrus, paper, stone, metals, pottery, vellum and wood - and was developed independently in different parts of the world.

Fig.1. Page from a 14th century Breviary, Cologne. Vellum is as fine as paper, and much more durable, which has aided the survival of documents before the development of printing in the 15th century. Note the fine original colours and gold decoration.

Writing seems to have been pioneered in Mesopotamia (modern Iraq) in the 4th millennium BC. In Europe, although some tablets with unintelligible markings were found in a pit at La Tartaria in Romania, dating from circa 4,500 BC, these are now seen as connected with cult activities. If this interpretation is accepted, no writing was employed in Europe until the rise of the Aegean civilisation of Bronze Age Greece and even then, the tablets in the scripts known as Linear A and Linear B (which date from circa 1600 BC and earlier) provide information that remains enigmatic.

In Britain, the first certain historical date is 55 BC, the year in which Julius Caesar crossed the Channel, writing a detailed account of his campaigns and descriptions of his adversaries. Where it has been possible to cross-check his accounts (for example at Alesia where the Gaulish leader Vercingetorix was finally besieged), they have been seen to be usefully accurate.

Fig.3. A piece of bone inscribed with the personal name "Aethili", found in excavations at the Dark Age citadel on the Mote of Mark, Kirkcudbrightshire in 1973.

Fig.4. Not all historical events are easily recognisable from documents - on this coin Julius Caesar (the elephant) is subduing Gaul (the snake) prior to providing Britain with her first historical date of 55 BC.

Doesn't history tell us enough without archaeology?

Since history is almost exclusively concerned with the written word there are limits to the information that it can provide. In many periods of the past, literacy was uncommon and reserved for a few sectors of society - typically (in the Western world, for example) priests and the rich. As a result history often strongly reflects the preoccupations of these groups and is generally uninformative about the rest of the population.

Many written records survived by chance and others exist only in copies that were made in later times; some exist only as fragments. Some written material was kept in libraries in Constantinople (Byzantium, now Istanbul) and became more widely available after the fall of the city to the Turks in 1453. There are, however, very few surviving original records of events in Britain during the Roman period or its immediate aftermath. Even where copies survive, information has sometimes been added or deleted by the copyist to serve a particular purpose, or perhaps to try to make sense of material that

seemed incorrect. It is often impossible to prove whether the record is reporting a true occurrence.

As a result there are many gaps in historical evidence, by period, or intent, type or survival. However, because of the differences in raw material, it is rarely possible for history and archaeology to provide evidence for the same aspects of society, even for periods with a large body of written material.

Archaeology is therefore of special importance in studying remote, non-literate or semi-literate periods for which there are few or no written records (see pre- and proto-history). Increasingly, archaeology is used to study aspects of life in well-documented periods that were simply not written about directly (for example, the daily life of ordinary people). Archaeology routinely throws light on aspects of the past on which documentary sources are largely silent, such as technology or types of everyday objects that were in use in particular communities.

What is meant by the terms prehistoric and protohistoric?

The word prehistoric means "before written history". Thus in those parts of Britain that were occupied by the Romans, the period before the arrival of Julius Caesar in 55 BC is regarded as prehistoric and everything after that is historic.

"Protohistoric" is sometimes used to mean a period when there was writing in other areas, but little or none in the one under scrutiny. In France, *protohistorique* means "at a time when there was writing somewhere" - making everything after about 3500 BC "protohistory".

In Britain "protohistoric" is used to mean a period when there were no local historical records, but when writers outside Britain were discussing events within it. It is usually employed with reference to the "Dark Ages" in the 5th to 7th centuries AD, but is sometimes also used for the later Iron Age, from the time of Julius Caesar's visit in 55 BC. In those parts of Britain not occupied by the Romans, however, there is little to distinguish the prehistoric from protohistoric, and other terms have been employed for specific periods and areas, such as "migration period" or "early Christian period".

How much archaeological

evidence survives?

As with historical records, the material that survives is largely a matter of chance; depending on the environment and human agency.

(a) In most British soils, organic material such as wood, leather and cloth does not survive except under very rare conditions. In very adverse conditions, even stonework may become friable. Organic materials can survive in stable, waterlogged conditions such as ditches, wells or bogs, or in extremely dry conditions (such as those which prevailed in Tutankhamen's tomb in Egypt), or in deep frost (in the case of the Iceman of the Alps).

(b) Some items were recycled when broken, or scattered over wide areas when no longer needed. Even when items were deliberately buried, they do not represent a cross-section of artefacts available. Grave goods, for example, must have been deliberately selected (the same types of objects are often found in many interments). Why they were selected is more conjectural (page 91).

(c) Modern life has also distorted the picture - most chance finds come to light through disturbance of the soil by building, ploughing or planting. In general terms, this happens less in remoter areas than in those that are densely populated. Some areas that are currently sparsely populated (such as Dartmoor or Orkney) were relatively densely settled in prehistory.

Fig.5. Part of Hadrian's Wall - preserved through its remoteness from developments over nearly two millennia.

Modern town centres with long histories of rebuilding often retain very little of their earliest phases. Conversely, early material can be preserved under the build-up of material which accumulates over the centuries. It is common for foundations to be constructed on the demolition layers of previous buildings (see page 47 stratigraphy).

(d) An imbalance in the evidence is also created by the distribution of people interested in archaeology. In areas where there are (or were) thriving archaeological and historical societies, local museums and perhaps university departments where archaeology is taught and researched, far more is generally noticed than in areas that have no such traditions. A few areas have thriving university departments that are concerned with overseas, theoretical or global studies and have little or no input in local matters. Some areas were subject to much interest from the 16th century onwards, but others have made up for an historical dearth of antiquarian interest through developing data bases for tourism and general cultural amenity. Commercial field units (excavators) similarly have varying input into the community (which may be based on time and money constraints).

How reliable is archaeological evidence?

Like historical material, archaeological evidence is of variable reliability, ranging from the very certain to the very shaky. Skill in making inferences, assumptions and deductions, and knowing how to interpret such material, is vital.

Very certain - technology. Analysis of materials used, the sources of the raw materials, and the technology needed to produce the finished result can show, for example, how pots were made, axes chipped or brooches enamelled.

Fairly certain - economics. Study of animal bones, seeds, pollen, or beetle wing cases can throw light on farming methods and the environment. Conclusions can be drawn about trade networks and routes, from raw materials that were transported far from their origins, or objects where the place of manufacture can be proven. Deductions may be made about specialised craft production, types of houses, and how settlement related to the landscape.

Less certain - social structure and organisation. Deductions in these areas tend to be more subjective and therefore inconclusive. For example, cemeteries containing both richly and poorly furnished graves could imply that the society had some degree of social stratification, but other explanations such as religious beliefs might also be valid. Similarly, a large building surrounded by smaller, similar structures, might suggest that the community had some kind of "head person". However, the substantial building might have been a temple or a communal meeting-place and - as is evident today - size, type or furnishings of a home may well not indicate the true power or wealth of its owner.

Shaky to very shaky indeed - beliefs, customs and matters of the mind. Ideas, philosophies, laws, beliefs, superstitions, political ideologies, literature, changing territorial boundaries, and (with a few rare exceptions provided by battle cemeteries) wars, can rarely be deduced from archaeological sources alone. For example, the remains of a post used as a may-pole, with its attendant folk songs, dances and recitations of traditional stories, might leave remains identical to a post used for tethering an animal or flying a flag.

Items placed in graves have been seen as implying a belief in the afterlife (ie seen as useful to the deceased in the future). However, Christian burials are typically unfurnished on the grounds that material goods were not seen as relevant to the type of afterlife expected. Grave goods may instead have sent particular messages to the living about the status of the deceased and/or the status and surplus wealth of the surviving relatives. Attila the Hun, for example, was noted for the understated nature of his conspicuous wealth, in contrast to that of his lieutenants (although his funeral is recorded as being very lavish and at least one of his homes was unusually well-equipped). Medieval bishops, however, were often interred with their rings and crosiers, apparently in contradiction to Christian belief. Rare exceptions where some inferences of belief can tentatively be suggested, concern sacrificial victims.

Surely we already have enough information about the past?

Fig.6. The disappearing past - the ruins of the Roman fort at Lympne, Kent, now no longer visible (from T. Wright, "The Celt, the Roman and the Saxon", 1861).

The remains of the past are non-renewable resources and it is accepted in law that we have a duty to preserve as much as possible for future generations (Chapter 8).

It is therefore held by many people to be important to know as much as possible so that informed judgements can be made about what to preserve and how to do so. This can create sensitive situations when there are conflicts involving new roads or buildings, wildlife, or religious beliefs.

Since study of the past has not been uniform in terms of area, region or types of remains, in some areas mistakes, inconsistencies and downright myths have been perpetuated about particular sites simply because there has been no pressing need to reappraise them. If a well-known antiquary or eminent local personage took interest in the site, or if it were mentioned in a little-known or misunderstood document, myths can arise about the importance, as well as the state of preservation and the exact nature of the monument or find. It is surprising how quickly knowledge is lost if not constantly reinforced and how quickly destruction can take place as a result.

Fig.7. Modern tile fragments set in concrete found at a
Roman villa site in Nottinghamshire and kept for 60 years
as an example of Roman mosaic.

Fig.8. Roman tesserae - one made from a piece of
datable, samian pottery, from the same site as in Fig.7.
that went unrecognised in the plough soil.

Why study the past?

Some of the reasons people give are closely related to political views, sociology, and psychology. I list a few reasons people have given me, in no particular order.

- By giving respect to the dead and their achievements society learns to have respect for the living and the future.

- To explore present problems in a detached way through analogy - today's multicultural society may have lessons to learn from similarly composed societies in the past.

- The pursuit can, if properly supervised, foster and train invaluable transferable skills at relatively little cost - observation, deduction, inference, assumption and abstract thought as well as imaginative reconstruction and lateral thinking.

- Archaeology fosters cooperation between many different disciplines in a common cause.

- To gain a sense of proportion about our own lives and times.

- Because it is intellectually challenging, often fun, and sometimes pure escapism.

- To get to the root of particular aspects of life today that may be based on tradition, outmoded or still relevant.

- To gain a feeling of security and "belonging" - to understand the basic underlying culture of the area in which we live (which may be thousands of miles from where our ancestors or families lived or live).

- To learn from past skills (organic farming is a good example of people effectively returning to the only methods available to our ancestors).

- Because, despite certain legal restrictions and controversies, the amateur or semi-professional can still make observations and discoveries that can push the subject along. Given that the subject is so wide, every experience or skill has the potential of being helpful.

- The width of the subject enables everyone - old, young, fit or disabled - to be involved or make a contribution.

Science helps archaeology - does archaeology ever help science?

The **Titanic**, arguably the most famous wreck in history, lies 4000m deep south-east of Newfoundland - too deep for divers. Remotely operated vehicles (ROVs) fitted with cameras have provided photographs of possessions on the seabed. They are, however, very expensive. Objects recovered from the wreck appear well preserved after over 75 years on the seabed, but once raised, the chlorides and sulphides corroding the metal alloys react with the air and decay is accelerated. Objects require to be transferred immediately to fresh water, and only removed long enough for photography and rapid examination.

The study is helping to advance the study of corrosion processes. The exploration of the **Titanic** cost millions of dollars, which was offset by the US government to test out equipment that could be used by the military.

How is data collected?

Methods improve as technology and knowledge progresses, and the resources are very diverse. Aerial photography, remote sensing, maps and crop marks, excavation, augering, and environmental sampling are outlined in Chapter 3.

All primary methods have their drawbacks and are only as good as their operators. Excavation, augering and many scientific tests involve the destruction of information (if the investigators do not meticulously record, store and make available to others their findings) or the material itself. The ethics and laws governing such activity are outlined in Chapter 8. Common sense and observation, as well as specialist knowledge and research are vital.

How do archaeologists spread information?

The results of archaeological research are published through a wide variety of agencies. These include national journals (published by national societies and which are sometimes period based - prehistoric, Roman, medieval etc); and local journals, which publish the results of work that is of regional interest. Bodies such as the Council for British Archaeology publish volumes of specialist reports or conference proceedings. Many studies are published as one-off volumes by commercial publishers, while others are published by local authorities or the developers who paid for the research. Word of mouth, TV programmes, archaeological magazines, books, and newspapers spread information to the general public.

Where are archaeologists employed?

People dealing with archaeological material as part of or all of their work can be employed in many different walks of life - museums, art galleries, journalism, publishing, television, county councils, state controlled bodies (such as English Heritage), Charitable Trusts, planning offices, building developments, surveying, commercial excavation and fieldwork units, schools and universities. Archaeologists may spend much of their time working indoors or outdoors in urban or rural situations, under water, deep underground in caves, or taking photographs from the air.

There is much cross-referencing between professions - archaeologists often consult specialists over individual finds (surgeons, veterinary surgeons or botanists over organic material, for example) and vice versa (the police consult archaeologists).

Figures are difficult to establish, but in 1993 around 2,200 people were employed in field archaeology, with around 860 permanent posts. Approximately 250 staff were employed in 2003 in the 21 University Departments currently included in the Research Ratings (RAE) for British Universities. Many thousands are involved in the heritage industry, museums, and other related areas.

*Fig.9. Some buildings have never been lost, such as the
"Old Work" at Wroxeter, Salop - the wall of the gym
attached to the bath building of the Roman town.*

Chapter Two

When did the study begin?

A lthough there is evidence that people in the remote past were curious about objects that they found, it was not until the 15th century that people began to take the type of serious interest that led to the present study.

How did modern archaeology develop?

Some ancient material has never been lost - the Colosseum in Rome simply fell out of use and was only slightly "robbed" or defaced over the centuries; the Roman remains in Bath were visible in the Dark Ages and the subject of an Anglo-Saxon poem entitled "The Ruin"; the pyramids still stand.

Scholars in Renaissance Italy first began to focus on the remains of Roman civilization that still stood after over a thousand years. Soon the rest of Europe followed the trend, focussing on periods of the past for which there was documentary evidence.

Within this intellectual framework, the study was founded in two very differing traditions - tomb or grave robbing, and scholarly interest. A clear distinction could be made from the start between treasure hunters and those who attempted to record meticulously and make reasoned inferences about the past. Ironically, the robbers were often supplying

Fig.10. The Colosseum and Arch of Constantine in Rome have never been "lost".

Fig.11. Raphael Fabretti was one of the pioneers of Roman archaeology - his "De Aquis et Aquaductibus Veteris Romae" (About water and aqueducts in ancient Rome) published in 1680 was a survey that has aided modern research.

buyers who held genuinely scholarly interests (the antiquaries).

Scholarly interest followed a number of different lines (generally speaking either in the arts or sciences).

For some, the development of Greek and Roman art and architecture was the most interesting aspect of the past.

Another strand of inquiry was motivated by the wish to find out more about the world in which the Bible was written. From this, interest developed in the "Old World" civilisations of the ancient Near East, such as Egypt or Assyria.

Other investigators were concerned with scientific development or with drawing parallels between "non-developed" societies in the past and in the present. From these developed the study of European prehistory.

Fig.12. A map from Fabretti's book, showing the aqueducts round Rome.

Who were the grave robbers and barrow diggers?

Fig.13. Victorian diggers at work, uncovering a kiln at Water Newton, Cambs (after Thomas Wright, 1861). Pictures such as these show how much of the past has been lost in the last 200 years alone.

People in the past often buried their dead with treasures or simple objects. In the late 18th and early 19th century, some British landowners would set a team of labourers to open as many prehistoric burial-mounds in a day as possible.

Few records were kept of what was found, but a step towards recording (and thus scientific excavation) was taken by two late 18th century diggers (Douglas and Faussett), both of whom were clergymen and knew one another.

James Douglas (1753-1819), (the more astute antiquary) made ground plans of the barrows he investigated and his **Nenia Britannica** is a landmark in British archaeology.

Bryan Faussett's (1720-1776) site diaries are fairly meticulous and accompanied by drawings and descriptions of the finds, and their positions in the graves. He did not publish his excavation of Anglo-Saxon burials in Kent, which he believed were Roman, but they were published (with his diary entries) by Charles Roach Smith in 1856.

Sir Richard Colt Hoare (1758-1838) and William Cunnington (1754-1810) attempted objectivity in their records, which were published in **Ancient Wiltshire**. They confined themselves to prehistoric barrows. "We speak from facts, not theory" wrote Sir Richard grandly, before lapsing into a gloriously subjective description of a skull, which "grinned horribly a ghastly smile".

Were there real archaeologists like Indiana Jones?

Some of the early pioneers of archaeological investigation led extremely colourful lives, full of adventure and danger.

Giovanni Belzoni (1778-1823) was originally a circus strong-man from Padua. He reached Egypt from England in 1815, intent on selling a hydraulic pump he had invented, to the pasha of Egypt, Mohammed Ali. Ali was not interested in the machine, so Belzoni began obtaining antiquities for the British consul-general. Belzoni thought big: moving giant statues and breaking open tombs to "rob the Egyptians of their papyri". Describing one of his adventures, he wrote: "After the exertion of entering into such a place, through a passage of fifty, a hundred, three hundred, or perhaps six hundred yards, nearly overcome, I sought a resting place, found one and contrived to sit, but when my weight bore on the body of an Egyptian, it crushed it like a band-box. I naturally had recourse to my hands to sustain my weight, but they found no better support; so that I sunk altogether among the broken mummies, with a crash of bones, rags and wooden cases, which raised such a dust as kept me motionless for a quarter of an hour, waiting till it subsided again...."

Austen Henry Layard (1817-1894) gave up studying law at the age of 22 in 1839, to become an explorer, hoping to reach Ceylon through Europe, the Near East and India.

Fig.14. Moving an Assyrian winged bull at Nimrud (from Layard, "Nineveh and its Remains", 1854). This illustration and Fig.15. show the immense scale on which sites were looted in the past.

22

Fig.15. Transporting the winged bull (from Layard, "Nineveh and its Remains", 1854).

Civil war in Mesopotamia changed his plans, so that after two years travelling in the most dangerous areas of Persia, Layard returned to Baghdad, robbed, barefoot and in rags. He excavated at Nimrud, financed by £60 from the British ambassador to the Ottoman Turkish Empire. Assisted by six workmen, he dug in two separate places on the mound and in less than 12 hours found two palaces, adorned with rich carvings.

Despite some strenuous local opposition, in 1846 the British Museum gave Layard £2000 to cover both the expenses of the team, and the cost of transporting his finds to England. He aimed to recover "the largest possible number of well-preserved objects of art at the least possible outlay of time and money".

His method was to dig trenches along the faces of the walls he found, exposing the sculptures, but leaving the interiors of the rooms undisturbed. Much was thus missed and/or destroyed, although excavators returned in the 1950s.

Layard's spectacular discoveries included winged bulls and reliefs now in the British Museum, frescoes, bronze helmets, and bowls. The Black Obelisk of Shalmaneser III mentioned an Israelite king, and was the first piece of independent evidence for

Are there still looters?

There have been a few major scandals in Britain involving the illicit looting of sites. The Thetford Treasure – a hoard of Roman silver spoons and other items from Norfolk - was found and concealed. Another incident occurred over an Iron Age temple site at Wanborough, Hampshire, a third involved the Roman bronze statuettes looted from Icklingham, Suffolk that turned up in the Ariadne galleries in New York, to where they had been exported illegally.

What was antiquarianism?

Fig.16. This drawing of an ancient Briton was published in 1803 in Lyttleton's "History of England", and was copied from an Elizabethan picture of a Pict.

events in the Bible established by archaeology.

In Britain the antiquaries were people (generally rich, male, and successful in other careers) whose scholarly interests extended to many other subjects as well as archaeology, such as local history, heraldry, architecture, languages and natural science. The period of antiquarianism lasted until around 1860, though the term "archaeology" was in use by the 18th century and major advances were made in the first half of the 19th century in establishing a frame-

Fig.17. An ancient British woman, from the same source as Fig.16.

Who were the British antiquaries?

Fig.18. Some antiquaries made good records - this plan shows the Neolithic chambered tomb at Stoney Littleton, Somerset (from T. Wright, "The Celt, the Roman and the Saxon", 1861).

Fig.19. William Camden, Elizabethan antiquary, from the frontispiece of Gibson's 1695 edition of "Britannia".

work for studying prehistory.

In Britain, the first antiquaries were Elizabethan, some of whom started long-lasting "myths" based on their best guesses at the time and with the data available.

John Leland (circa 1506-1552) was appointed state antiquary (the first and last), by Henry VIII. He recorded such diverse monuments as Hadrian's Wall, Offa's Dyke and the Devil's Arrows. He went mad in the process and died with his book unpublished, although it was used and copied by later workers.

William Camden (1555-1623), was the most prominent Elizabethan antiquary - he was persuaded by the map-maker Ortelius to put his knowledge of antiquities into a book, **Britannia**.

This was arranged in regions according to the

tribes known (from written sources such as Caesar) to have occupied Britain in Roman times. It gave an account of the known antiquities as a type of touring guide. The first edition was in Latin, in 1586, but English translations soon followed. After his death it was enlarged by later writers such as Edmund Gibson, whose version was published in 1695. By the end of the 18th century it had grown to three massive folios, and was still being consulted in the time of Queen Victoria. Camden was one of the first to identify Iron Age coins for what they were and study Anglo-Saxon mints. Stonehenge defeated him - he pronounced it an *insana substructio* ("mad construction").

John Aubrey advanced the recording of field monuments in the 17th century through his book **Monumenta Britannica** (British Monuments). This was also used by later antiquaries but not published until 1978.

Edward Lhwyd (1660-1708), a Welsh scholar, studied and classified the Celtic languages. He introduced the Celts to the British perception of the past, thus widening the arena from the Classical world. He was the first to record carefully Dark Age inscriptions in Wales, and explained that flint arrowheads were not made by elves to injure cattle (the commonly-held explanation) but were projectile points used by ancient Britons in the way American Indians used them in his own time.

William Stukeley (1687-1765) gave up medicine for the Church and started writing "vegetable sermons" - the works of God as illustrated by vegetables. He was obsessed by druids and held parties in which the (often) noble partygoers were addressed by such titles as "My Lord Archdruid Bathurst". He concluded that Stonehenge and Avebury were built by the druids.

Despite the theatricals (or more probably because of the interest they fuelled) he produced some significant work. Between 1719 and 1725 he surveyed Stonehenge and Avebury very precisely, and travelled Britain from Dorset to Hadrian's Wall, illustrating the monuments that he saw with his own careful drawings that appeared in **Itinerarium Curiosum**, an archaeological travel book first published in 1724.

Stukeley noticed the importance of cropmarks, which are widely used today, and argued that monuments needed to be studied in the wider landscape. He was convinced that invasions from the Continent must have occurred during prehistory (see invasion hypothesis page 34).

Fig.21. Stonehenge in a 19th century engraving (from Wright, 1861) before some stones were re-erected.

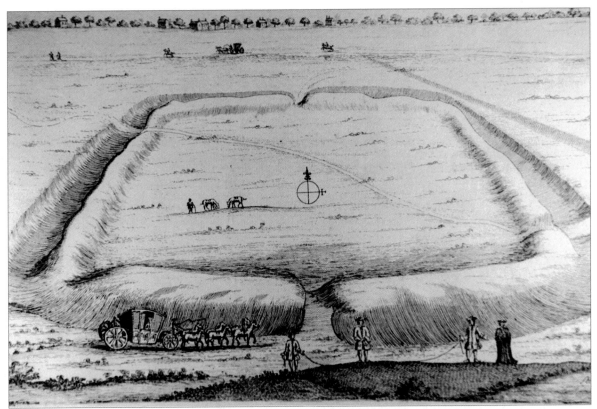

Fig.20. Remains of the Roman fort (Caesar's Camp) at Hounslow, Middlesex, from "Itinerarium Curiosum", drawn by William Stukeley in 1723.

Can contemporary societies throw light on ancient society?

Particularly in the 19th century, scholars studied contemporaneous societies that seemed to have a similar lifestyle to that in prehistoric times. "Stone Age" societies were observed to see how they fashioned stone tools, built houses, or viewed art. This process (comparative ethnology), fell out of favour when it was realised that similar results in lifestyle might be triggered by very different situations.

The idea was given a new "spin" by Lewis Binford and others in the later 1970s and 80s. In order to apply his conclusions to the study of people in the Palaeolithic, Binford studied the Inuit (Esquimaux) to see what dictated the variations in assemblages of flint tools. Similarly, the context in which the famous stone heads of Easter Island were erected was seen to have relevance to the building of Stonehenge. Although perhaps useful in studying how objects were made, ethnoarchaeology was criticised because it assumed that societies always respond in the same way to the

Who were the pioneers

of modern archaeology?

same stimuli. Much controversy exists in this area.

The most celebrated archaeological pioneers often came from careers in totally different subjects. Their expertise moved antiquarians into the modern world. They include General Pitt Rivers, Sir Arthur Evans, Sir Flinders Petrie, Sir Mortimer Wheeler, Oscar Montelius, Heinrich Schliemann and many others. In the recent past many breakthroughs were made by people who are still alive, but have been omitted from this book to avoid disappointment

Who carried out the first

archaeological excavation?

caused by lack of space.

As with other aspects of archaeology, digging took a long time to develop from the looting of sites for treasure and collectors' items, to a scientific study. Its development was not uniform, following different paths at different times in different regions.

General Pitt Rivers (1827-1900) developed methods of excavation after becoming interested in

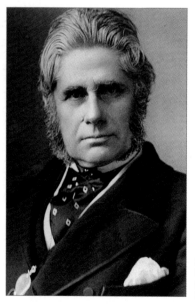

artefacts through the study of the rifle.

Having inherited huge estates on Cranborne Chase in Wiltshire, he excavated in a military manner, publishing the results in substantial volumes. Everything he saw was meticulously recorded, whether he understood it or not, which has enabled later scholars to reinterpret as knowledge increases. The exact position of finds in relation to changes in soil colouration, and features such as ditches were noted and drawn. Individual potshards, human skulls and other bones were precisely drawn with the help of a gadget he devised for taking exact measurements. Pitt Rivers' excavation reports have a modern look, with tables and statistics.

Sir Mortimer Wheeler (1890-1976) revived Pitt Rivers' methods in excavations at the Roman fort of *Segontium*, Caernarvon, in North Wales in the early 1920s. Although fashions have changed and Wheeler's grid excavation method (later developed in the East) is no longer fashionable, relatively little has changed in basic methodology (despite developments in recording and conservation methods).

Sir Flinders Petrie (1853-1942) made a survey of the Egyptian pyramids which is still regarded as reliable (despite his lack of formal education he was a skilled draughtsman and surveyor). Like Pitt Rivers,

Fig.22. General Pitt Rivers, innovative and prominent excavator, from the frontispiece to "Excavations at Bokerley Dyke and Wansdyke", ("Excavations in Cranborne Chase", vol III, 1892).

Fig.23. The "Palace of Minos" at Knossos, Crete (thought to be the "Labyrinth" of Greek myth, excavated by Sir Arthur Evans, as it was in 1974.

Petrie was meticulous in his recording and insisted that small, common items were as important as the more spectacular, refusing to throw away beads, potshards and broken tools as previous excavators had done. He also stressed the importance of studying groups of material, and of using typologies to arrange sequences when absolute dating was lacking for the material he worked on.

Petrie briefly introduced his methods to the Near East, where they were taken up at the end of the 19th century by such men as Robert Koldewey at Babylon and Walter Andrae at Asshur. The use of stratified pottery in the Near East was developed by George Reisner in Palestine (1908-10) and Leonard Woolley at Carchemish in Syria (1911-14).

Arthur Evans (1851-1941) carried on the work begun by Schliemann (page 101) in the investigation of the Bronze Age civilization of Greece. He excavated what he called "The Palace of Minos" at Knossos in Crete and developed excavation tech-

How are sites

uncovered or discovered?

Fig.25. The erosion of the past - the Roman fort at Walton Castle, Suffolk, has now been totally eroded by the sea since the 1780s when this print was made.

niques there.

Sites are found by accident, by natural forces or by deliberate investigation. Accidental finds can occur during building works, road works, quarrying or the ploughing of areas not previously cultivated; through metal detecting or through the agencies of nature - erosion of cliffs, river banks, sand dunes and even through the activities of rabbits or moles.

Unusual climatic conditions can reveal sites - dry summers often reveal crop marks, which may not recur for decades. Unless covered by later building or heavy deposits, very ancient sites can be found a few inches below the turf, and on high, exposed sites such as rocky hilltops, erosion can eventually remove all traces of occupation.

The Neolithic village of Skara Brae (in Orkney) is

an outstanding example of a major discovery, which came to light through natural agencies.

In 1850, a storm blew the sand away from a midden and some stone-built huts. Some desultory digging followed, and a few huts were exposed. In 1925 another violent storm stripped yet more huts and it subsequently became apparent that here was the best-preserved Neolithic settlement in Britain - so well-preserved that its excavator Professor Gordon Childe, did not initially believe its age. Even the furniture was made of stone. It is now under threat from changing sea conditions.

In Shetland, the Viking site at Jarlshof first came to light after a heavy storm in 1896, when walls were revealed. Subsequently it was discovered that the site was occupied more or less continuously from the

Fig.26. A house in the Neolithic village of Skara Brae, Orkney was protected by sand for millennia and is now under threat from the sea.

How do things and
sites get lost?

Neolithic to the 17th century, with only short breaks.

Many remains are buried as a result of natural forces. The Roman town of Pompeii was covered in ash, by volcanic eruption; ancient Egyptian, tombs by sand; and many sites by the sea or coastal erosion.

Some such sites may be time capsules (page 62). However, most buried British sites are not intact, having over the centuries been stripped for re-usable building materials. This thrift often results in foundations in towns standing on remains of earlier demolished buildings that may be several metres under the present surfaces.

Once reduced to ground level, airborne leaves, sand or soil may cover the remains, eventually forming soil. Animals such as moles, and the casting worms, *allolobophora longa* or *allolobophora nocturna*, constantly bring earth to the surface. Solifluction (soil-slip) can result in earth sliding from higher ground to cover features at lower levels.

Why are the things broken?

Objects found on archaeological settlement sites are usually broken because they were discarded as rubbish or were lost and not retrieved. Subsequently, the action of the weather or activities such as ploughing or building works often damages material.

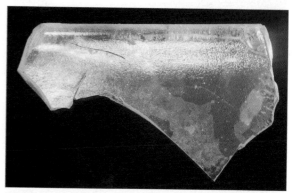

Fig.27. Tiny fragment of Rhenish drinking glass from an excavation at Barton in Fabis; badly damaged but still recognisable and having an attractive patina.

Why are things not broken?

Sometimes objects survive intact by chance, but the most common occurrence is when they were buried with the dead and have therefore been protected by the grave itself. It is a salutary fact that a large number of intact objects that come onto the open market must have originated in graves.

Fig.28. Roman North African ware, 5th century AD.

Fig.29. Roman glass vessel of the 2nd century AD, preserved almost certainly by being buried in a grave.

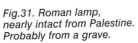

Fig.30. Roman jug with damaged lip - a common occurrence when pots are hit by the plough.

Fig.31. Roman lamp, nearly intact from Palestine. Probably from a grave.

Is archaeology subject to fashion or social trends?

Archaeology, like all other subjects, is both constrained and driven by the attitudes, values, perceptions and interests of the day. The way people view and interpret evidence depends, amongst other things, on the way they have been taught to view it; the way they have "rebelled" against such teaching and what factors society currently sees as important. Although much data concerning technology is unassailable, the more subjective interpretations do change. This tendency was particularly marked in the late 20th century (pages 77-80 and below, the invasion hypothesis).

Although archaeologists are usually aware of some of their prejudices and biases, their thinking is also coloured by more subliminal attitudes and perceptions: they are, in short, trapped in their own time as much as everybody else. New techniques for studying material are often seized on with great enthusiasm, before flaws or drawbacks are discovered. The modern Western world is currently aware of the need to live harmoniously in a multi-cultural society. There is therefore a strong interest in "ethnicity" and how it can be recognised archaeologically, as well as a desire to avoid "imposing" ethnic, racial or cultural stereotypes on past societies. This is exemplified by the current debate as to whether the term "Celts" should be used of the Iron Age Britons.

What is the invasion hypothesis?

This assumes that material found in British prehistoric contexts which is identical to material on the Continent, implies that there were cross-Channel migrations. Proof of hostilities, violence or even intent to invade is difficult to find but the theory has notably been favoured at times when Britain was itself engaged in or preoccupied with invasions of other territories (ie in the Victorian period and during the World Wars). In times of peace and economic prosperity the same evidence tends to be explained as the result of trade. It is of course possible that both these explanations are valid.

The invasion hypothesis was closely connected in Victorian thought to Darwin's theory of evolution and diffusionism (page 65).

Fig.24. The Roman invasion of Britain was a well-documented reality but note the scythed chariot, a long-enduring myth about the Britons (from Miller's "History of the Anglo-Saxons", 1850) that is not borne out by archaeology.

Are there any more finds left to be found?

Although there is no doubt that destruction of sites has increased in the past 30 years, every year so many finds are made and reported in the press that is impossible to mention even a small proportion in this book. The type of site that can be detected is changing due to modern technology, so that large numbers of badly damaged remains are now being recognised.

One outstanding example of a totally unexpected major find was "Seahenge" - a surviving timber circle similar to prehistoric stone examples. A local man found a Bronze Age axe on the eroded peat beds of a beach in north Norfolk that were exposed by the retreating tides. A circle of blackened timber posts surrounded a tree trunk, apparently still retaining branches. Subsequent investigation showed that the "branches" were the roots of a 2 ton oak which had been turned upside down. It appeared to have been lowered into place using a rope made of honeysuckle. The central oak was shown by dendrochronology (page 69) to have been felled in the spring of 2050 BC. The surrounding posts were not spaced out with gaps, as in a stone circle, but would have presented a continuous wall with only a small gap under a forked post providing entry. This had eventually been deliberately blocked. The suggestion that this might have had a ritual purpose of some kind has gained favour.

What are the different branches of archaeology?

Several branches are evolving as technology develops (Chapter 5) - the most prominent are field archaeology, landscape studies, industrial, environmental, scientific, underwater and theoretical archaeology. The latter includes a number of specialist branches that have evolved over the last three decades. They are more concerned with approaches than practical matters and have produced an overwhelming number of technical terms. Conservation and museum studies are closely allied subjects, along with heritage studies and management.

Chapter 3

Methods of retrieval of data

The many methods of data retrieval can be divided into non-invasive (generally non-destructive), invasive (generally destructive), and scientific analysis of artefacts or sample material (which may be destructive or non-destructive).

What is a desk-top survey?

This is an appraisal of a site and its potential carried out from an office, normally using a computer database and library archives. It is usually a first stop when researching ahead of building developments or for private or academic study purposes. The drawbacks are that computer-based archives are only as good as the entries on them. Many databases in Britain have been lamentably reduced or neglected through lack of time and money as all resources have been directed to archaeological material under immediate threat of destruction.

Information can therefore be garbled or out of date, with many omissions and mistakes made by inexperienced, unmotivated and/or unpaid operators.

Surveys need to be supplemented by, and cross-referenced from, the original sources. This has the drawback of being time-consuming since academic journals and other reports are often not available from the same library. Furthermore, despite efforts to reduce the backlog of unpublished material in museums, many primary records remain hand-written field notes or card files and some have been detached from the objects to which they refer.

What investigative techniques

are non-invasive?

Studying aerial photographs, maps and other documentary material, fieldwalking and landscape studies, remote sensing and experimental archaeology rarely do damage to archaeological material or features.

What do old maps show?

Old maps are a valuable source of information for such features as vanished or heavily-defaced burial mounds, ditches, banks, or buildings. They can provide place names and fieldnames, which relate to now vanished archaeological features. In addition, estate maps and terriers (tenancy maps showing the ownership of fields) can show long vanished strip fields and boundaries. The existence of these features can be used to eliminate other explanations as well as to identify sites.

Are place names of significance?

Field, street and place names often relate to structures, occupations or land use in the past. The study of place names is complex, since names may not be derived from the words they most resemble in modern English - it is necessary to search records for the oldest form of the name before it can be interpreted. Several excellent reference books exist, from which I take a few examples. Field (and settlement) names incorporating the word "street" imply the existence of a Roman road. Roman or other buildings are sometimes suggested by names such as "stony field" or "red field" (on account of Roman tiles and bricks found there). The word "low" can refer to an ancient burial mound, and "dyke" to an ancient ditch (not to be confused for the Scottish word for wall). Names such as "Pinfold" point to the former location of enclosures where stray animals were penned.

What is fieldwalking?

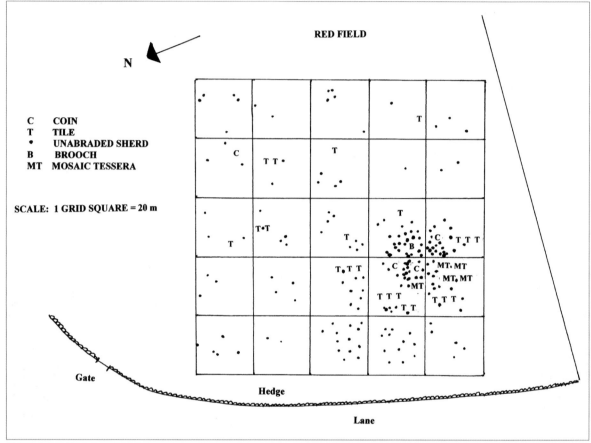

Fig.32. Fieldwalking - typical distribution of finds plotted on a grid, from which deductions can sometimes be made about locations of sites.

This is a method of detecting sites by collecting and mapping finds lying on the surface of ploughed fields.

Method: lay out lines or grids at 1m intervals with string in a field or part of a field. As the researchers walk across the land each find - flint, pot, bone, glass, metal etc - is noted and its position plotted on a base map. This can be very time-consuming and sometimes, if large areas are involved, sampling is carried out to provide a statistically meaningful result.

The benefits: concentrations of some material may denote a nearby site and the type of find may indicate its extent, age, and type (Roman military or prehistoric domestic, for example).

The down side: objects may have been brought to the fields from elsewhere through normal farming processes. For example, the modern practice of taking sugar beet to a central point of collection before shaking off excess soil can remove objects far from their place of origin. Objects from many sites and periods can frustratingly and misleadingly lead to incorrect deductions about an area. Additionally, animals and natural causes such as streams or slump may distort the findings, though it has recently been demonstrated that, contrary to popular belief, finds do not migrate far due to plough action since they are continually moved back and forth in the same area.

What is remote sensing?

Remote sensing is the term used to describe a number of methods of detecting sites that are not normally visible by walking over the land. There are two main methods, aerial photography and geophysical prospecting.

What are the principles of aerial photography?

Features may be visible from the air but not from ground level. When the sun is low, minor bumps and hollows will cast shadows, perhaps indicating where walls or ditches lie. These features may also be accentuated by drifting snow or leaves, which gather in hollows.

Fig.33. Aerial photograph of Prehistoric settlement.

Fig.34. Aerial photograph of medieval settlement.

Snow and frost often melt more rapidly where an underground wall retains heat, and conversely will lie longer above ditches.

Features are also shown up on occasion after ploughing, when the tops of walls may be scattered and appear as lighter patches of soil. Such soil may be all that is left.

Cropmarks are caused by the different growth capacities of vegetation. Where the ground has been disturbed and water is retained, roots can penetrate deeply, causing crops to grow taller and greener. Where roots are inhibited by stones in walls, plants are often shorter and/or paler.

Similarly, where the vegetation dries out and/or dies over walls, parch marks may be found. Cropmarks are very unpredictable, and often short-lived; times of drought are usually fruitful for researchers, so the timing of reconnaissance flights is crucial. The main drawback of aerial photography is that interpretation may be difficult on a complex site or where modern ploughing methods have confused the picture. In addition, a ditch which has been filled with stones from the fields may resemble a wall; or a wall that has been robbed out may be filled with leaf mould which supports good crop growth.

In modern aerial photography different types of film produce different results, and infra-red photography has proved very successful. Most aerial photography is done from low-flying aircraft and the resultant oblique views need to be "justified" to counter distortions. Vertical photography from fixed air balloons has also been employed.

Fig.35. Tomen-y-Mur, Gwynedd, Roman military ludus
(small arena for armed combat training) revealed by snow
in early 1970s.

Fig.36. Diagram to show how crop growth
is affected by underground features.

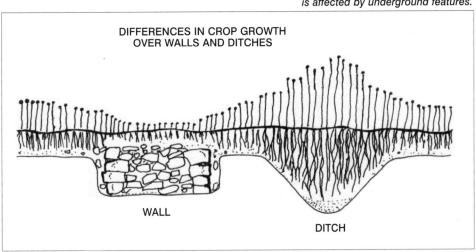

DIFFERENCES IN CROP GROWTH
OVER WALLS AND DITCHES

WALL

DITCH

What are the main methods
of geophysical prospecting?

Geophysical prospecting is the detection of buried features using scientific instruments.

Metal detectors, which were initially developed for locating land mines, have gained increasing popularity with hobbyists in Britain since the late 1960s.

Although modern metal detectors have reached heights of ever-increasing sophistication, and can distinguish between different types of metal, most have relatively low depth penetration on small individual targets (ie the most effective modern metal detectors can achieve a depth of about 12in or so in "non-mineralised" ground).

Many of the recent "Treasure Reports" and press publicity demonstrate the contribution of metal detectors to archaeology.

In addition, it is possible - when using a metal detector - to assess the amount of iron or mineralization present on a particular part of a site; such material can indicate habitation or an area that has seen above-normal activity.

Pulse Induction detectors are deeper-seeking but usually used by hobby metal detectorists only on the

Fig.37. Metal detecting finds - Roman rings showing signs of corrosion.

wet sand of beaches due to their sensitivity to iron. They are sometimes used within archaeology when there is a need to recover all metallic items on a site.

The resistivity meter calculates the amount of resistance an electrical current meets when passed through ground.

The current passes fairly readily through loose or damp soil, but has more difficulty with dry or compact features such as walls. In modern geophysical prospecting a pair of fixed probes are inserted into any convenient place near the test area, as a "control" and the amount of resistance encountered by

Fig.38. Iron latch lifters found in excavation at Barton in Fabis, well preserved but corroded.

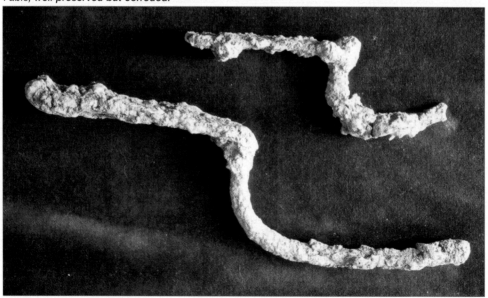

Fig.39. Geophysical prospecting with a resistivity meter at Fortingal, Perthshire, in 1999.

Fig.40. The plot of Roman underground features revealed by resistivity at Barton-in-Fabis, Notts, in 2000. The nature of these has not been determined. At the one point where scatter was apparently minimal, excavation revealed wall footings (Fig.41.) of unproven date but associated with Roman material. Note the blue circular features along the bottom of the printout and linear features across the area, which reflect the churned up ground where cattle congregate at troughs and gates.

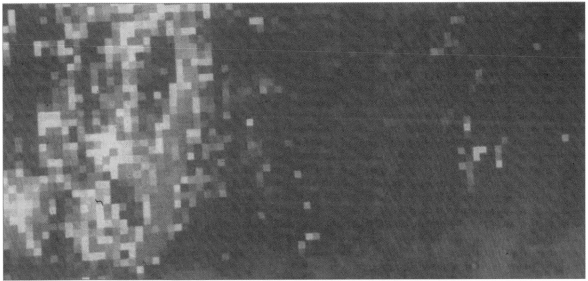

"mobile" probes is measured against it. Normally, a 20m grid is laid out and readings taken at 1m intervals by inserting the mobile probes into the ground. Under good conditions, merely resting the probes on the ground is sufficient. The data is logged by computer and transferred for analysis to a dedicated computer programme.

The resultant plot shows up features such as walls and ditches, although the same provisos operate as for crop marks - high resistance might mean a ditch has been infilled with stone, and low resistance might denote a robbed-out wall. When tested at one site in Nottinghamshire the results were as shown in Figs.40-42.

The shape of the features underground may, nonetheless, be sufficiently stereotypical to indicate the type of site without further invasive work.

Magnetometers measure magnetic variations in the soil - the most popular is the automatic fluxgate gradiometer. Magnetometry has the advantage that no probes need to be pushed into the ground. The disadvantage is that it is susceptible to any form of magnetism, including the natural magnetism in the operator's body. All metal objects such as keys, spectacles, watches, coins, and clothing with metal fasteners or decorations must be discarded. This usually means planning ahead with care! Magnetometers are particularly successful in detecting pottery kilns or hearths, where there is a strong magnetic field. They have the advantage of being faster and easier to operate (once the somewhat tedious business of calibration has been done) than resistivity meters but the latter is often more rewarding in Britain.

Ground penetrating radar measures signals that are "bounced" off buried features. While the resultant plots can indicate the depth of ditches or heights of walls (impossible with the other methods), the interpretation requires great skill and the method is currently under development.

Phosphate analysis - organic waste (for example, where cattle or sheep were once penned) can result in a higher level of phosphates in the soil. This can lead to the discovery of sites as well as giving indications of land use.

GIS - Geographical Information Systems - are used for the precise location and documentation of geographical and (by extension) archaeological features using computers. They constitute essential tools in plotting and studying settlements in terms of distribution and location. Maps can be digitised and layers of spatial data may be put into the database (for example contours, land-use, and the location of sites) allowing landscapes to be viewed in different ways. It is possible to see the relationship of sites to sea levels or water level in the past.

Surveys of sites can now be carried out very precisely through the use of a "Total Station" that pinpoints positions using satellites.

How did they do that?

This sort of speculation is common in respect of both huge edifices such as Stonehenge and minutely detailed works of art. The question "how was it built?" is usually asked about prehistoric monuments such as standing stones, giant mounds such as Silbury Hill in Wiltshire, and some of the hill forts of the Iron Age.

The level of technology available as well as the organisation of society either politically or through religious beliefs, is often the key. The use of the wheel or water power, for example, may have been available. The strength of oxen, so rarely seen today, is often underestimated. Clearly, many different techniques were used for building in wood, stone or brick, and were dictated by the level of technology available. The skill of carpenters and stonemasons should never be underestimated, despite the simplicity of the tools they employed.

Sometimes the only way to determine how something was made is to reproduce it, and by trial and error achieve the desired result (experimental archaeology page 78).

Fig.41. One of the four trenches cut in 2001 at Barton in Fabis was sited at the point where resistivity showed little disturbance over a much disturbed wall footing.

Fig.42. A second trial trench revealed this scatter of rubble gravel and stones that could not be investigated in the time available. The site is very disturbed, as shown by the "modern" field drain which, like the putative Roman wall footings, was overlain by a layer of gravel, just visible in this picture.

What are the main invasive techniques in archaeology?

Excavation, augering and some sampling involve the removal of material (see below).

What are the pros and cons of augering?

An auger is a hand-held or mechanically-operated drill, which takes a core of material from the earth. Originally used in geology, it is now widely used in archaeology to test quickly whether there is significant material under ground. The method will show the stratigraphy at the point the core is taken and obviously the date or type of any objects within the core may be studied.

The drawbacks are that it breaks material (stories of the auger drilling through otherwise intact mosaic floors or whole pots are not unknown) and finds may fall into different levels of stratigraphy, thus potentially making a nonsense of the site for future archaeologists. When auger holes are taken at metre intervals a site may be seriously damaged and some people consider that this is only justifiable if destruction of the site is unavoidable, as an aid to planning more detailed investigation.

Excavation - what are the pros and cons?

Excavation is the pursuit most commonly associated with archaeologists, though this will be decreasingly the case due to new legislation (Chapter 10), and the need to conserve resources. Excavation is expensive and time-consuming, and requires considerable organisation and a wide variety of resources and personnel. Pages 47-55 briefly explain a few of the less technical terms which need to be understood for full evaluation of site reports and other desktop surveys.

Fig.43. Trowelling at Keighton deserted medieval village, Nottingham University campus, in 1999.

Is archaeological work dangerous?

The main dangers to life and limb are during excavations, where inevitably equipment can pose potential threats as on building sites or in gardening. Another danger may be the transmission of diseases, which can occur long after the material has left the site.

Archaeologists have been killed by the collapse of trenches and when climbing or visiting remote sites. Excavators have been seriously injured by misused picks, mattocks and other tools; by falling down trenches; and by chemicals used.

Before any fieldwork it is necessary to carry out a risk evaluation, and excavations must have qualified first-aiders as part of the team. Investigations under-water or deep underground obviously have their own dangers.

Fig.44. The author about to be winched 400ft under Beeston Castle, Cheshire in the mid 1970s where potholers were investigating the dried up well. Ralegh Radford (the celebrated excavator of King Arthur's tomb, Glastonbury) is also pictured.

What is stratigraphy?

This is the study of the different layers (strata) of soil and the order and way in which they have been deposited. The way in which stratigraphy builds up is exemplified by newspapers pushed through the letterbox during a holiday period. In theory on return the earliest will be at the bottom and the latest at the top, but some may have been pushed through with greater force than others and may have fallen to the side, out of sequence. The golden rule in excavation is to remove the most recent layer first, and to keep everything from that layer separate from the one underneath. In practice, the sequence will have been disturbed by later workings. Highly complex stratigraphy can result - over a hundred layers have been recorded in a metre's depth. Recognising different strata and features requires long and arduous on-site training.

Inverted stratigraphy (where the oldest material is at the top) is rare. It happens if, for example, the side of a large pit, wall or ditch collapses.

What is a Wheeler grid?

This term is used to describe a system of excavation developed by Sir Mortimer Wheeler which involves a pattern of excavated squares or "boxes" separated by balks. Measurements from pegs at the intersections can be used to pinpoint finds and features. As the excavation advances, the balks can be separately excavated and recorded, to amalgamate boxes into larger areas.

The purpose of this system was to provide as many sections (sides to the trenches) as possible, as an aid to site interpretation. It is particularly useful where there are deep deposits of complex layers, and relatively clearly defined structures. Modern technology (for example the "total station") theoretically obviates the necessity for this method.

What is a section?

A section is a vertical plan of the layers and features that have been dug through, drawn from the side or end of the trench. It is customary to excavate only half the contents of a pit or posthole in the first instance, leaving a vertical section that can be drawn. A section can act as a cross-check for work already done and as a two-dimensional image of material removed.

Fig.45. A section through the strong room cellar in the Roman fort at Caernarvon, showing how coins were used to date the sequence (after Wheeler, "Segontium and the Roman Occupation of Wales", 1922).

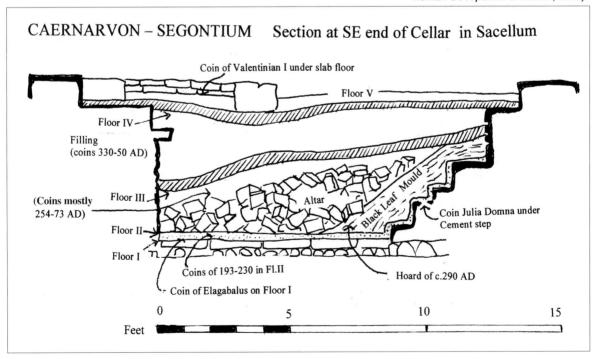

CAERNARVON – SEGONTIUM   Section at SE end of Cellar in Sacellum

Coin of Valentinian I under slab floor

Floor V

Floor IV

Filling
(coins 330-50 AD)

(Coins mostly 254-73 AD)   Floor III

Altar

Black Leaf Mould

Coin Julia Domna under
Cement step

Floor II

Floor I

Coins of 193-230 in Fl.II

Coin of Elagabalus on Floor I

Hoard of c.290 AD

0   5   10   15

Feet

Fig.46. A section through a Roman ditch at Barton-in-Fabis, in 2000, showing tiles and opus signinum (Roman flooring) in the filling.

What is Schnitt excavation?

This method of excavation was developed by German archaeologists such as Gerhard Bersu, and involves excavating in spits. It is sometimes called the "planum" method and is used where stratigraphy is not clear. It requires excavating down to each horizontal surface, noting changes in soil, and keeping the finds from each soil context separately. Interpretation takes place off site, where computers have greatly aided such methods of recording.

What is a post hole?

When a post rots *in situ*, the decayed wood eventually forms earth. If the structure burnt down, the post-hole may be filled with charcoal. Where the post has been removed deliberately, the hole left will (usually) be filled with earth of a different colour and consistency from the soil into which it was dug. The resultant feature is termed a "post hole".

What is area excavation?

Fig.47. Sedgeford, Norfolk, area excavation
(note the water sprinklers necessary in the hot weather).

Immediately after the Second World War excavators such as W.F. Grimes were already favouring the investigation of larger areas, but area excavation became much more popular in the late 20th century when it was necessary to examine large expanses rapidly in advance of building development. The technique is particularly useful where there is no large build-up of stratigraphy, as on many rural sites and gravel deposits. Sections are still drawn across ditches and other features.

What are soil shadows?

Soil shadows usually occur when organic material has totally decomposed, leaving a mark in the soil. Bodies sometimes decay totally leaving only a stain that is vaguely human-shaped. At Sutton Hoo, Suffolk, the excavators found what they termed Anglo-Saxon "sandmen" - areas of compacted and differently coloured sand, where bodies had been. One showed a man who had been buried in a running position with similarly insubstantial remains of a plough.

Fig.48. Sedgeford, Norfolk, excavation of a waterlogged area only yards from the very different conditions in Fig.47.

What is a robber trench?

A robber trench occurs where building materials have been taken for recycling and has no implication of illegality. This was most common with stone walls and foundations, though wooden buildings were also deliberately demolished. Plans of buildings may survive as roughly dug trenches where the walls once stood, infilled with random material the "robbers" discarded, as well as a natural build up of soil.

What is ghosting?

Sometimes, signs of a feature appear at a higher level in the soil. In the case of a wall, for example, the soil above it may be compacted differently from that in the adjacent area, or may contain flecks of mortar or rubble, possibly brought to the surface by worm action. Sometimes, the contents of a deep pit will settle and overlying soil will dip into the hollow. Such a phenomenon, in excavation, is known as ghosting.

What is a spoil tip?

The material, usually soil, which has been removed during excavation and from which sample material and finds have been removed, is termed "spoil".

What is a midden?

A midden is a rubbish heap, usually piled up outside a dwelling at a time when there was no systematic collection of rubbish. The alternative methods of rubbish disposal in antiquity were by burial in a pit, or spreading on the fields with manure.

Middens are very informative since they often contain artefacts that provide evidence of lifestyle.

Some of the earliest middens in Britain are heaps of shells collected by Mesolithic coastal dwellers. A Neolithic culture in Scandinavia was formerly named the "Kitchen Midden Culture" since it was first recognised from middens.

On aerial photographs middens may be confused with, for example, burials of farm animals or remains of clay or marl digging.

Why do archaeologists make records, and how?

The purpose of recording is to enable excavators and researchers in the future to interpret what has been found and compare the findings with others; every site is unique, within its general category. If the excavators have open minds, they should not be making judgements until all the information has been collected. Within broad limits, much may be known before excavation starts, but meticulous records enable the best possible results to be achieved and erroneous preconceived ideas or expectations to be eliminated.

If the recording is scrupulously accurate, the work will be useful long after it has been completed. General Pitt Rivers did not understand the significance of a timber feature he found in a Neolithic earthen long barrow at Wor Barrow in Dorset. Sixty years later it was possible to see that he had found a type of structure that had by that time been identified as a long mortuary enclosure, in use for burials before the barrow was put up.

Recording takes many forms, starting with the pre-excavation survey of the site, through to the recording of the sections, the layers, the structures, the features and the finds; and their context and the relationship of one context to another. It ends with the ongoing analysis of material in the lab or museum that may never end as each new generation of scholars or students find fresh approaches.

Fig.49. Wor Barrow, a Neolithic long barrow, before excavation by Pitt Rivers.

Fig.50. Wor Barrow during excavation - the "pyramids" were Pitt Rivers' control balks and his recording was so meticulous that the site could be re-interpreted in the 20th century. (From "Excavations in Cranborne Chase", vol IV, 1898).

Fig.51. Planning using a planning frame, Keighton,
Nottingham University campus.

Fig.52. Drawing a section at
Keighton, Nottingham University
campus, in 1999.

What is a context?

In the past most recording was done in terms of layers (strata), which were given individual numbers, prefaced by a code indicating the trench in which they were situated. In modern excavation it is more customary to assign a context number for each feature that is encountered - not just layers but walls, post-holes and so on. The record notes the relationship of each context to the others adjacent. On some sites this can build into a dauntingly complex data base. However, each excavation and excavation team is different, and many variations on the theme may be encountered.

What happens to finds
on an excavation?

Broadly speaking, as they come to light, artefacts are placed in a finds tray that contains two labels. These bear the code number of the context in which the find has been made - post hole/pit/layer/ditch etc. When the tray is full or the context dug out, the tray is taken to the finds hut, where "first aid" conservation is given, if necessary. Artefacts are washed (in the case of pottery, stone and bone) or brushed (in the case of metal), being at all times kept with a context label.

If necessary, further finds labels are created as material is then sorted into category - pottery, bone, buildings materials etc. These are bagged up, usually in polythene "minigrip" bags, and labelled with the type of content, site code, and context number. Unusual items are termed "small finds" and each is assigned an individual number and entered in a finds' register with details of its context and description, usually with a sketch drawing. They are usually stored separately, unless laboratory conservation is required.

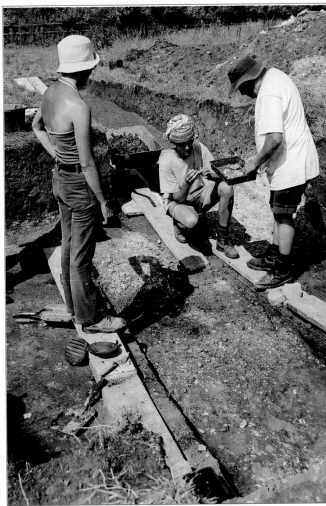

Fig.53. Preliminary inspection of a finds tray at Sedgeford, Norfolk.

Fig.54. The finds "hut" at Sedgeford in 2003.

By this means material can be checked against the onsite records kept by the supervisors. This is important not only for "posterity" but when material is dispersed to various laboratories for analysis over the years, or put on display. It should be possible at any stage in the future to pinpoint the exact find spot of each and every tiny potsherd, in relation to every other find and every feature or layer on the site. Use of modern computerised surveying equipment enables each context and each find, if necessary, to be pinpointed to an exceptionally high level of accuracy.

How are finds processed?

Many finds need little more than simple brushing carried out in the field, but each object must be treated individually according to its material makeup, condition and the prevailing circumstances. Some fragile objects are lifted in a matrix of earth so that investigation can be carried out in the laboratory. Cleaning by conservators is usually prefaced by X-raying (to determine the extent of the object under the corrosion, or the presence of inlays, etc). Ideally, conservation work is kept to a minimum to ensure the survival of the object, and cleaning is only carried out when it is essential to reveal details of ornament, etc.

Finds are then subjected to what may be many years of tests and study in the laboratory and museums before being drawn and/or photographed for publication. This process normally takes many times the period spent on site, and is by far the most costly pursuit, for which reason it has been notoriously the most neglected in the past.

How are artefacts analysed?

A wide range of techniques are used for studying the composition of objects, depending on the type of material and the information sought. Nearly all methods of examining metals involve exciting the atoms of which they are composed and identifying them from the way they behave. In these studies the identification of trace elements is particularly important, since they vary and can be used to pinpoint the source. A few methods are outlined below - X-ray fluorescence analysis, Scanning Electron Microprobe Analysis, Inductively-coupled Plasma Atomic Emission Spectrometry, Optical Emission Spectrometry and Petrology. Analysis of artefacts and inorganic material requires different approaches.

In **X-ray fluorescence analysis** (known as XRF) a beam of X-rays bombard the electrons in the inner shells of the atoms, which are driven up to the surface before returning. This uses up a measurable amount of energy and the elements present in the sample can be identified. It is particularly useful in examining pottery, glass and glazes, but is also used for metals. It is usually more helpful to clean the surface of metal, or drill a core sample, since the penetration of the X-rays is up to a millimetre for pottery and glass, but much more superficial for metals, and the surface often does not give a true reflection of the composition.

Scanning Electron Microprobe analysis (known as SEM) works along similar lines to XRF. An "electron gun" bombards the surface with a beam of electrons in a vacuum. Material for this has to be carefully prepared and mounted up as thin sections (thin slices of the material, which allow light through to reveal mineral composition) or as flat, carbon or gold-coated samples. The advantages of the method are (1) an area as small as one thousandth of a millimetre can be examined and (2) different layers in a sample can be separately examined.

Inductively-coupled Plasma Atomic Emission Spectrometry (known as ICP-MS) is a comparatively reliable and inexpensive method of analysis. The accuracy is plus or minus 5%, and only 10mg of material is needed for analysis.

Ion Beam Analysis is a group of techniques, of which the most important is **Proton-Induced X-ray Emission** (known as PIXE). This depends on using a beam of protons from a particle accelerator to excite the emission of X-rays. It is used for very small area analysis, and for thin layers such as pigments or solders used in ornamental metalworking.

Neutron Activation Analysis (known as NAA) requires a nuclear reactor - the objects irradiated remain radioactive for many years (this is not a popular technique!).

Isotopic Analysis is used for the chemical identification of elements.

Petrology is used for the identification of rock sources. It can be used to examine objects made of stone (from tools to free-standing sculptures), and for objects that have stone in their composition (such as the clays used to make pottery). The normal method of studying stone and clays is by cutting a thin section. In the case of pottery, although the clay may sometimes be distinguishable by eye, many clays are the same in appearance, and it is only the presence of particles of rocks or minerals that can pinpoint the source. Sometimes microscopic fossils can help the investigator find the source of the minerals.

Magnetometry is used in land and underwater prospecting. It was used to detect the remains of the Méduse, a French frigate lost in 1816 off the coast of Mauritania. Here the instrument used was a nuclear resonance magnetometer, developed by the French Atomic Energy Commission.

Side-scan sonar is employed on sites in shallower water. It is horizontally-sweeping radar, which shows as shadow projections on the seabed, including wrecks. Using fibre optic and digital imaging, wrecks at considerable depths can be scanned. With the aid of sub-bottom profilers objects buried beneath the seabed can be detected within a few centimetres precision - this includes metal objects, wooden boats and submerged tree trunks.

What can be learned from artefact analysis?

The method of manufacture can provide information about technological skills. It is usually fairly easy to determine by eye whether a metal object has been cast, and the casting method used. It will also be fairly clear if there is evidence of plating, inlaying, the addition of enamel and so on. Similarly with pottery it is fairly easy to determine whether it is hand-made, made on a slow or a fast wheel, moulded, stamped or rouletted. It is often possible to determine by eye that a stone is not native to its find spot.

For more precise study, scientific methods of examination can determine not only how objects were made and the sophistication of the technology, but also the sources of the raw materials.

Petrology has been used to show how the Anglo-Saxons and Normans sometimes traded building stone over very long distances. It has demonstrated that the bluestones of Stonehenge originated in the Preseli Mountains of South Wales, and that the great ceremonial whetstone from the Anglo-Saxon royal burial at Sutton Hoo, Suffolk, came from south-west Scotland.

Fig.55. A Neolithic axe from the Great Langdale axe factory, Cumbria, broken in manufacture.

Fig.56. Bronze Age ingot ready for metallurgical analysis.

Very recently, petrology has been used to show how usually, but not always, early medieval sculptures were made of local stone. The analysis of prehistoric stone axes has revealed a complex network of long-distance trade in Neolithic Britain, with axe factories such as Great Langdale in Cumbria, or Tievebulliagh in Antrim trading throughout Britain.

The analysis of pottery has demonstrated how far prehistoric pots were traded - from Cornwall to Wiltshire in both the Neolithic and the Iron Age, for example. A destructive technique known as thin-sectioning has been used to identify the Mediterranean sources of Roman amphorae (wine storage jars) and Dark Age bowls in France.

The analysis of metals has similarly been used to trace the source of the raw materials and the place where objects were made. A good example, concerns the "King and Prince of Stonehenge". These recently discovered burials near Stonehenge (dating from circa 2400 BC) were found to be of an archer and (probably) his son. Copper found in the graves came from the Continent, and analysis of tooth enamel suggested that the "king" had spent his childhood in central Europe.

Chapter 4

How do you know
what date it is?

People often have difficulty believing that
dates can be found for even tiny fragments of
certain objects, but sometimes cannot be
found for quite large sites (for example Dark Age or
Iron Age sites). This is usually due to the random
survival of material combined with the available
dating methods.

Are dates certain?

There are two types of date - relative and
absolute. Many historical dates are absolute - for
example, it is certain that the First World War started
in 1914, that the battle of Hastings took place on 14
October 1066 and the Roman city of Pompeii was
engulfed in August AD 79.

Archaeological dates are usually far less certain
even though there are now numerous ways of determining dates for manufacture or destruction of
material. Many types of material can be dated only to
general periods - often the reigns of emperors or
kings, if coins or inscriptions are credibly and closely
associated with them. Many absolute dating methods
are achieved by scientific techniques of which the
most common are radio-carbon (for use on organic
material such as wood or bone); luminescence (for
pottery and burnt flints, for example), dendrochronology (for use on wood): potassium-argon
dating (used with fossils), and archaeomagnetic dating which is often cross-referenced with other
methods.

In excavations of sites with few surviving objects
it is often only possible to establish that a particular
feature or find came before or after another fixed or
presumed event (see *terminus post quem* and *terminus
ante quem*, and date brackets, page 61).

Fig.57. A house in Pompeii, Italy, engulfed in AD 79.

What are the main sources of dates for archaeological material?

Apart from scientifically produced examples, dates may be found on coins, or inscriptions on a variety of objects such as pots, building foundation slabs, ornamental or commemorative sculpture or grave stones. Archaeologists rarely find written documents, though outstanding exceptions to this rule are the tablets from the Roman site of Vindolanda near Hadrian's Wall, or the scrolls from the Villa of the Papyrii in Herculaneum. Pottery types are particularly important since pots were subject to change that can be cross referenced with other datable material.

Some coins can be dated through changes in weights and fineness. Most coins can be dated to the reign of the person who issued them, and often more closely. Roman coins and inscriptions can sometimes be dated to a particular month due to the method of dating which referred to the number of times a ruler had been hailed emperor and/or had the power of consul or tribune conferred. Translating such "dates" can be complex.

A method used in the absence of written or scientific dating, is typology. The presence of dated or datable material does not necessarily "date" the site, however, since objects may have originated elsewhere or had a long currency before being lost.

60

What is meant by terminus ante quem (taq)

and terminus post quem (tpq)?

These terms mean, respectively, the date before which and after which an event could not have happened. For example if a coin of 1850 were found under an expanse of undisturbed concrete, that surface could not have been laid down before the date the coin was minted and 1850 would be the terminus ante quem (terminal point before which the floor could have been laid down). Conversely, if it were known from documentary evidence that the floor had been laid down in 1945, anything that happened above it or to it (new flooring, layers of dirt, holes cut through it and so on), must have happened after that date. The year 1945 would be the terminus post quem for material under the floor. Obviously, objects found above the concrete might be many thousands of years older than the floor, having been brought from elsewhere, but the events (including bringing the ancient material to the site) could not be earlier.

The taq and tpq are used in excavation to provide general dates for layers or features, and to build up a relative sequence for events (see stratigraphy).

What is a date bracket?

In many situations it is impossible to put exact dates on either features or objects, but a terminus post quem and ante quem can be achieved. The intervening period is known as a date bracket. Cumbersome phrases such as that quoted in the Introduction - "the destruction level is datable to after the third quarter of the 1st century AD but does not post-date the later Hadrianic period" is an example of this.

What do BC, AD and BP stand for?

The system of dating in much of the modern world takes the traditional date of the birth of Christ (0) as a starting point. Hence dates BC are before the birth of Christ and those AD (Anno Domini - "In the year of Our Lord") are after Christ's birth. The system was developed by an Anglo-Saxon monk, the Venerable Bede, around the beginning of the 8th century, in a book called **De Tempore Ratione**.

Bede correlated other schemes of dating with his own, which was rapidly adopted in Europe, though not immediately used on objects or inscriptions. The idea of dating coins spread from the Islamic world (where coins were dated in terms of years after the Hijrah, Mohammed's Flight to Mecca - AD 622 under Bede's system). The first coins with an AD date were struck in 1166 in Spain, where Islamic influence was strong.

The expression BP means before present, which is taken as 1950 (see radio carbon dating, page 69).

What is a time capsule?

Fig.58. A street in Pompeii, engulfed in AD 79.

Some assemblages of material relate to a particular point in time when "everything stopped". Good examples are wrecks and natural disaster areas such as Pompeii and Herculaneum or the deliberately preserved collection at the Todai-ji in Japan. They may represent a cross section of life or only one aspect of it, and can sometimes be pinpointed very precisely. The scholarly worth of the objects is that they were in current use and had not been subjected to the random effects of having been thrown away or simply lost. Comparison with other material outside such a time capsule can help identify and date other sites.

The Roman town of Pompeii was engulfed in AD 79, leaving many intact houses and streets, since some inhabitants had not fled. Décor, design and furniture as well as scrolls were hermetically sealed in some rooms. Amongst the finds was a crate of pottery, fresh from the factory. The distinctive form has helped provide dates on other sites where this pottery has been found in close relationship with other material. The date for the disaster is known from a number of sources including two letters written by the younger Pliny whose uncle, the elder Pliny, died from asphyxiation near the town.

The Vasa, a Swedish flagship that went down in Stockholm harbour, was located after a five-year search. It was so well preserved that it could be lifted using holes under the ship made by pressure jet, through which wires could be passed. The vessel was lifted to the surface in 1961, after 333 years submerged. When it was lifted, the hull was filled with a metre of thick black mud which yielded 14,000 objects, made of wood, metal, fabric, glass, leather, and pottery. Wool only had to be put out to dry, but leather was freeze dried. The sails were a particular problem, as they were as fragile as wet newspaper.

What is typology?

Typology is the study of the way objects developed over a period of time, in style, manufacture and usage. It was fundamental in the organisation of material into the Three Age System (page 64) - the Stone, Bronze and Iron Ages. Typology was pioneered in the 19th century by the Swedish archaeologist Oscar Montelius. He noticed that a series of railway carriages could be arranged in the order in which they were produced, through observing the successive technical improvements. This was in line with 19th century ideas about evolution and progress, and the principle was applied to the arrangement of Bronze Age axes that could be shown to have developed by stages until they could be improved technically no further - the stage known as functional stasis.

The simpler the object, the sooner it reaches functional stasis; there is a limit to what can be done to improve shears or chisels, for example. This system of typology was used to provide relative dates for objects - if there was a fixed date at some point or points in the sequence, the stages of development could be slotted in.

Unfortunately, progress does not often take place at a steady rate, and some stages could have lasted much longer than others. Typology was gradually replaced by the development of scientific dating methods, but in the absence of other evidence the technique can still be useful, particularly in the study of pottery or art. Its main drawback is that objects often start simply, become more complex and then go through a period of degeneration - the early and late stages can be misleadingly similar.

What is a Skeuomorph?

Some features displayed on an object may once have served a practical function, but are retained as non-functioning ornamental details. Bronze Age axes, for example, sometimes have a raised crescent on the side, which denotes the original loop through which a cord was passed to tie the axe on to the handle. Fake stitching on "plastic" leather goods such as briefcases, or fixed buckles on shoes and decorative exterior window shutters, are modern examples.

Who invented the terms Stone Age,

Bronze Age and Iron Age

(the Three Age System)?

The concept of the Stone, Bronze and Iron Ages, was refined by Christian Thomsen, curator of the National Museum of Denmark in Copenhagen. Faced with over a thousand artefacts to arrange in some kind of order, he abandoned the traditional idea of categorising displays according to function and shape. Instead, using logic, he argued that stone implements must have been used before the invention of metalworking. This, he argued, must have been followed by a period when both stone and bronze were used, both later being supplanted by iron for most edged tools and weapons.

Under this scheme, the modern world is still in the Iron Age, although steel is also used for edge tools.

Thomsen's scheme was developed by Jens Worsaae who arranged Danish burial mounds in sequence. In 1842 Worsaae published **Danmarks Oldtid** (Ancient Denmark) which was translated in 1849 into **The Primeval Antiquities of Denmark**. It gave an account of the prehistory of Denmark that was based on the Three Age System, which, by the 1860s, was fairly universally followed in Europe.

In Britain the scheme was taken up by Sir John Lubbock (Lord Avebury) whose **Prehistoric Times** went through many editions until his death in 1913. Lubbock divided the Stone Age into an Old (Palaeolithic) and New (Neolithic) in the first, 1865, edition.

How were dates assigned to periods

(such as early prehistory) which did not

generate their own dating systems?

Having placed objects in a logical order of production (above) and shown that some must have predated historical events, scholars still had no idea how long "prehistory" had lasted. The vast time span between the first hominids and the present day remained largely inspired guesswork, until the advent of scientific methods of dating after the Second World War and changes in public opinion. The issue shared problems in public perception with Charles Darwin's theory of evolution (and a related concept - diffusionism) since it appeared to contradict the biblical account of how God created the world in the space of a few days. The possibility that the Biblical Adam had evolved from animals rather than being created in an instant, was held unthinkable. The idea that reason was a sin (since using reason was seen as questioning the works of God)

further hampered scientific development.

James Ussher (1581-1656) Archbishop of Armagh, made a series of calculations based on information in the Bible to work out a chronology for the Old Testament. Ussher calculated that the Creation took place in 4004 BC.

Dr. John Lightfoot using the same source, worked out that Adam was created at 9am on 23 October in that year.

At the end of the 17th century, a London apothecary and antique dealer called Conyers, noticed a stone axe associated with elephant bones during work at Gray's Inn Lane in London. He suggested that the tool had been made at a time when Britons did not have knowledge of metal. When it was pointed out that elephants had been brought to Britain by the invading Roman army in the time of Claudius, he accepted this explanation.

In 1800, John Frere wrote to the Society of Antiquaries of London, drawing attention to some flint implements (in fact, what are now known as Lower Palaeolithic Acheulian hand axes) found at Hoxne, in Suffolk, in association with the bones of extinct animals. He argued that they were "fabricated and used by a people who had not the use of metals....the situation which these weapons were found may tempt us to refer them to a very remote period indeed, even beyond that of the present world". Religious orthodoxy explained such finds and the discovery of the fossils of extinct animals as the remains of creatures drowned in Noah's Flood.

Subsequently, the different fossils in different strata of rock were explained by the suggestion that the biblical story of Noah's Flood was only the last of a series of similar events (the Catastrophe Theory).

In 1838, a French customs official, Jacques Boucher de Crevecoeur de Perthes, found some axes with the bones of extinct animals in the gravels of the Somme at Abbeville. In a three-volume work published in 1847, he convinced learned opinion in France that these axes were older than the Flood. His ideas were subsequently also accepted in Britain, with the discovery of flint implements and the bones of extinct animals under a layer of stalagmite at Windmill Hill Cave in Brixham.

On 2 June 1859, Sir John Evans announced to the Society of Antiquaries in London that "Man [humans] peopled Britain in a period of antiquity remote beyond any of which we have found traces".

It was not until the early years of the 20th century that a date was established for the Ice Age - Baron Louis Gerhard de Geer studied varves laid down annually by glacial melt waters, calculating that the last Ice Age ended 9,000 years ago.

What was the theory of evolution?

Publicly aired in 1871, the theory of evolution presupposed a long time span for the existence of human beings during which they evolved from other primates. Despite the controversies that surrounded it, some Victorians extended Darwin's ideas about natural evolution to other aspects of life, arguing that society evolved in the same way that animals did, and that artefacts too underwent a process of evolution (typology, page 63).

An English anthropologist, E.B. Tylor, set out a view of "social evolution" in 1889 which proclaimed: "Human institutions, like stratified rocks, succeed each other in series, substantially uniform over the Globe, independent of what seem the comparatively superficial differences of race and language, but shaped by similar human nature".

Tylor and others studied the evolution of separate elements in human cultures, not the holistic picture. In the 1870s Lewis Henry Morgan defined a three-stage evolution of human society, which he termed "ethnical periods" and which proceeded from Savagery, through Barbarism to Civilisation. Karl Marx and Friedrich Engels developed the scheme by introducing such concepts as a slave-owning stage.

In the evolutionary scheme, the same inventions were seen to have occurred in different societies at the point at which they had reached the same stage of development (ie the same inventions could be made independently in different parts of the world at different times).

This theory was countered by diffusionism.

What is diffusionism?

Under this theory, inventions and new ideas are seen to have happened only once, and spread out from their point of origin like ripples on a pond. The concept was taken up by the Australian prehistorian, Gordon Childe, who argued that there had been a

"Neolithic revolution". He saw farming as having been invented in the ancient Near East soon after the end of the Ice Age, and to have spread thence through Europe until it eventually reached Britain.

Can dates be cross-referenced
with other areas?

Oscar Montelius used fixed dates from Egypt as a starting point for cross-referencing with other cultures. The method depends on the existence of imported material that shows such similarity to that in areas where written records exist, that it can be assumed to be roughly contemporaneous.

Until the 1950s this was the only method available for calculating the date of Neolithic and Bronze Age sites in Britain. Given the obvious difficulties in making deductions, it is perhaps surprising that scientific dating methods have shown that, although the Neolithic was previously seen to begin much later than it did, the dates for its end and for the Bronze and Iron Ages were not far out.

Occasionally cross references to dates can be made when, for example, astronomical phenomena such as comets were noted in the records of two different societies.

What is an archaeological culture?

Using ideas borrowed from anthropologists, Gordon Childe (1892-1957) argued that material remains are "fossilised human behaviour" and that if one group of people shared the same types of buildings, settlements, pottery, tools, and economy that were not shared by another adjacent group, then this should be regarded as a "culture".

Under his arguments, it followed that the people in one culture might also have shared traits such as customs, political structures and beliefs that have left no material traces. This approach to archaeology became known later as "cultural historical" archaeology or "culture history".

Cultures have frequently been named after definitive objects within them, so that archaeological literature sometimes refers to the Beaker people when there is no proof that the people using this type of pottery had much else in common beyond the availability of similar possessions and skills. Both the charm and the flaw in this theory is that it cannot be tested at present. Its chief problem is that it is difficult not to assume subconsciously that such cultures were real rather than conceptual. When applied to modern society (in which, obviously, other factors may operate) it does not work - for example, choice of particular styles of furniture, crockery and so on does not prove or even imply common political views.

What is an archaeological horizon?

A horizon occurs in archaeological terminology when a series of identical traits or artefacts are found over a wide area for a definable period of time. These occurrences can be found in different cultures, but provide a date bracket linking the sites on which they are found.

What Were the Dark Ages?

Fig.59. Possible Dark Age fort at Little Dunagoil, Bute - many sites have little to show of this period and may belong to many periods. Part of their charm lies in the (often) scenic locations.

The term usually means a time about which very little is known historically, but which lies between two well documented eras. The Greek "Dark Ages" were between the collapse of the Bronze Age civilisations of the Minoans and Mycenaeans and the emergence of Classical Greece. In Britain, "Dark Age" is usually used to describe the period from the withdrawal of Roman troops in the early 5th century and the arrival of Christianity and written records following the mission of St Augustine in 597 to the Kentish court. Other date brackets and terms are also used as knowledge is expanded.

These periods often produce stories about heroes (Jason, Hercules and so on from Greece, and King Arthur in Britain) that may well have been based on real people but exaggerated later.

Fig.60. The antiquarian imagination at work on the Dark Ages - the conversion of the English by St Augustine (AD 597). Note Stonehenge in the background and the pensive pagan priest with his dagger (frontispiece to Miller's "History of the Anglo-Saxons", 1850)

What were the Middle Ages in the middle of?

Fig.61. Medieval castle at Threave, Dumfries and Galloway, preserved partly by its remote location and delightfully romantic setting.

The terms "Middle Ages" and "medieval" were first used in the 16th century to cover the period between the Classical Roman world (sometimes called "Antiquity") and the Renaissance (the "rebirth" or revival of Classical learning in the late 15th and 16th centuries). Traditionally in Britain, the Middle Ages have been arbitrarily taken as between 1066 (the Norman Conquest) to 1485 (Richard III defeated by Henry Tudor). However, when I was a student the Dark Ages were bypassed in favour of starting the Middle Ages at the end of the Roman period in Britain. On the Continent this would include the Migration Period and in Scotland and Ireland, the Early Christian period. There are clearly many ways of defining this term, depending on the standpoint taken.

What scientific dating methods are there?

The most common are radio-carbon, luminescence, archaeomagnetic (remanent magnetic), dendrochronology and potassium-argon dating. These can be applied to different materials and are detailed in Chapter 9. Each method has drawbacks and advantages and some are non-destructive, while others require the material to be destroyed and therefore must be used with caution.

Virtually all these methods are expensive and highly complex. None is infallible.

Radiocarbon dating is the best-known method of scientific dating. Although any organic material can be used in radiocarbon dating, twigs or nuts are best because of their short growing season. Charcoal from large trees is less reliable, because of the long growing life and, of course, structural timbers might have been around for a long time after the tree was felled and re-used in buildings. Usually around 10-20g of charcoal is needed for a sample, whereas for bone 100-500g is required. If AMS is used, (see below) only about 1/100th of these quantities are needed.

The technique depends on the fact that radioactive emissions from carbon start to reduce at the death of the organism until they are half strength. This, the "half-life" of the carbon isotope, is now fixed at 5730 plus or minus 40 years (originally this was calculated as 5568 years). In theory, by measuring the amount of radioactivity in a sample it is possible to say when the organism died, as far back as 70,000 years ago. For the sake of simplicity, radio-carbon dates are measured from a theoretical date of 1950, and are given as BP (before present), meaning "before 1950". It was first thought that the decay was taking place at a steady rate, but it was found that tree-ring dates (see below) were sometimes at variance with the radiocarbon dates. This led to the creation of a "calibration curve" in which "radiocarbon years" and "calendrical years" were adjusted when it became apparent that dates before 1000 BC underestimated calendrical years.

Accelerator mass spectrometry (AMS) has been developed since the 1980s and has refined radio-carbon dating since it compares the concentration of C14 to that in a normal isotope C12. It is much quicker, and can provide dates from before 40,000 years ago. Dates have been extended even further back recently by sampling marine corals, which can be compared with tree-ring dates and enable a calibration curve to be established back to 30,000 BC. Radiocarbon dates are expressed with a statistical estimate of error (the standard deviation), expressed as a number of years preceded by a + over - sign. Thus, if the date were cited as 4000 plus or minus 35 BP, there is a 68% chance that the actual date is between 3965 and 4035, and a 90% chance that it is between 3930 and 4070 before the present. It is usual to quote dates within the bracket of two standard deviations.

In giving dates, it is also usual to give the abbreviated name of the laboratory carrying out the measurement, and the sample number.

Dendrochronology or tree-ring dating is one of the most reliable methods of arriving at dates. Trees acquire annual growth rings - clearly visible from

Fig.62. Chart showing tree-ring links.

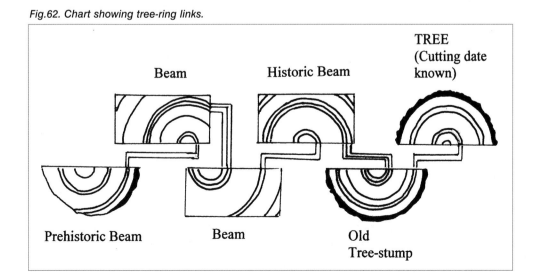

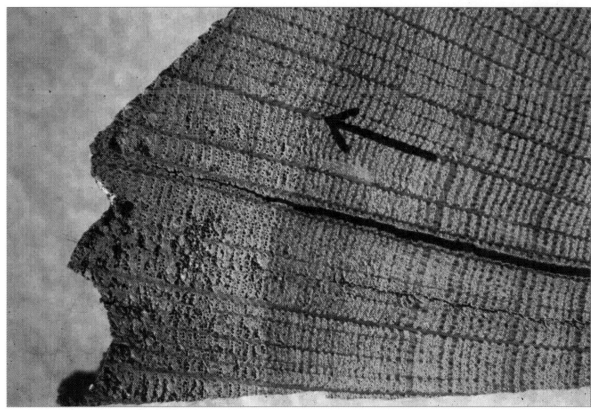

Fig.63. Section through beam, showing tree rings.

felled branches and trunks. The growth rings are dependent on climatic variation, and the rings are wider (or denser, depending on species) in some years than in others.

The pattern of growth over a period (rather than the exact dimensions of each ring) can be correlated between species and areas. The value of tree-ring dating was first appreciated in America in the 18th century, when the Rev. Cutler counted 463 growth rings on a tree growing on an Indian burial mound, and deduced the burial must have pre-dated Columbus (1492).

The technique was developed in the 20th century, when the role of climate was evaluated in a study of tree-rings in Arizona and New Mexico. Using timbers from pueblo villages where the arid climate had led to their preservation, a tree-ring sequence was worked out back to the 4th century BC.

In 1954 it was discovered that the bristlecone pine was the oldest living thing on the planet - some examples living to 4,000 years. By linking living trees back to old trunks a tree-ring sequence was worked out back to 6700 BC. In North-West Europe a similar sequence using oaks, has been linked to examples of trunks found in peat bogs, and in Germany, a sequence that uses pines, refers back to almost 10,000 BC.

A date can only be established with certainty, however, if all the sapwood is preserved. Where this is not totally preserved, a guess has to be made about how many years may be missing. There are problems also with re-used timbers, but sometimes cross checks can be made when the date of construction of a building is known.

Dendrochronology has been particularly useful in the dating of medieval buildings and other structures. At Coppergate, York, it was shown that the majority of houses were built with timbers felled in AD 975. At Alchester, near Oxford, it was shown that the timber fort was built in AD 44, one year after the Claudian invasion.

A timber bridge on the site of the early monastery at Clonmacnoise, Co Offaly, was shown to have been constructed in AD 804 or slightly later, and dendro-dating has been used to show that the tidal mill at Nendrum, Co Down was the earliest known in Europe, having been constructed in the summer of AD 619.

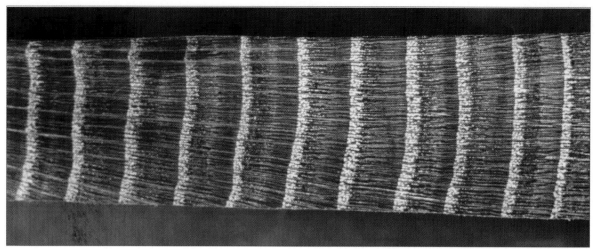

Fig.64. Section through beam, showing tree rings.

Luminescence Dating is used to date crystalline substances that have been exposed to strong heat. Originally used to date pottery, it is now used for a variety of other materials, including burnt flints. Samples are heated to release the electrons that have accumulated since they were fired, as they emit light in proportion to how many are present.

Natural sediments that have been exposed to the sun and then buried also retain evidence of radiation. **Optical dating** has proved particularly useful for dating deposits of sand. It has successfully shown that the ancestors of the aborigines arrived in Australia over 50,000 years ago. Unlike radiocarbon dating, there is no need to employ a calibration curve. It is not always very precise, but can be used on material in museum collections where contamination is unlikely to have taken place. A related technique, **Electron Spin Resonance**, is used to date teeth.

Archaeomagnetic dating (remanent magnetic dating) is concerned with the migration of magnetic north round the North Pole (it moves both up and down and from side to side, with a fluctuating magnetic field). Grains of iron oxide are contained in soil and clay, losing their magnetic alignment when heated to above 650 degrees Centigrade. Once cool, they align themselves on the current magnetic North. This alignment is maintained until they are re-heated to a similar level. So long as the exact alignment of the sample is recorded in the field, it can be aligned on the same axis in the laboratory, and then compared with the present one.

Potassium-argon dating has been used for dating the oldest human fossils in East Africa. Like carbon, potassium contains some radioactive isotopes, notably potassium 40 which decays into calcium and argon (which is released when volcanic rocks are being formed, but trapped in them as they harden). It can be released in the laboratory and its radioactivity measured. Its half-life is 1,250 million years, and is therefore useful for dating at periods when radiocarbon is valueless, and in areas where there are volcanic rocks. Dates for early hominids were found because layers containing fossil bones and artefacts were sandwiched between layers of volcanic deposits of lava. The date of "Lucy" a very early hominid from Kenya was seen to be 3,180,000 years ago by this method.

Fission-track dating is also dependent on volcanic eruptions and involves counting tracks left in glassy minerals (such as obsidian) by the fission of uranium-238.

Microscopy can show how objects were used through patterns of wear. Microscopes can further the study of techniques of decoration - for example, to indicate variations in decoration such as the use of the same stamp rather than two very similar ones.

Chapter 5

Approaches to Archaeology

Partly through historical accident, partly through availability of technology, and partly through scholarly dissatisfaction, a number of branches and approaches to the subject have evolved.

What are the main branches

of archaeology?

1. Field Archaeology - work undertaken primarily outdoors (not necessarily in the countryside) rather than in the museum, laboratory or library. It is generally concerned with recovering material for the first time, although some aspects are concerned with reappraisal of known facts. The best-known type of field archaeology is excavation, but a great deal is also done non-destructively with fieldwalking, surveying, studying crop marks and using new technology (pages 38-45). It is usually the first or second stage in a full-scale investigation (often concurrently with archival and library search). Commercial field units now dominate this activity and are especially constrained by money and time.

2. Industrial archaeology - the term was coined to include "above ground archaeology" since it was acknowledged that simply being buried was not a good reason for separate categorisation. Industrial archaeology initially comprised the study of remains from the Industrial Revolution, but has come to encompass studies of machines, mills, waterways, factories etc.

Fig.65. Industrial archaeology - an exhibit at Newark Air Museum, Notts.

Archaeology of the future?
A World War II "pillbox" in Rutland.

Fig.66. Industrial archaeology -
a windmill in Lincolnshire.

Fig.67. Flotation in progress.

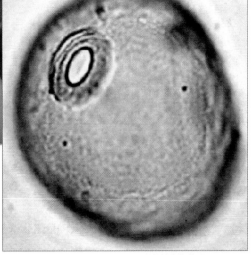

Fig.68. Magnified grain of cereal pollen.

3. Environmental archaeology is concerned with reconstructing the natural environment and subsistence economy of past societies. It is now a very important area of archaeological research in its own right. To understand how societies functioned in the past it is now held necessary to reconstruct the world in which they operated - the climate, the landscape, the natural plant cover, the course of rivers, water supplies, the wildlife, and the domesticated fauna and flora. Geologists, geomorphologists, biologists, botanists, zoologists and a number of other specialists are involved in creating an overview of the ecosystem.

(a) Plant remains are often difficult to see with the naked eye, yet are very important for studying environment for they represent a major element in the diet of a great many living things. The most common source of plant remains comprises sediments from the bottom of ditches or watercourses. These are sorted out from the rest of the material by passing the soil through sieves and by flotation in tanks.

• The smallest plant remains are particles of pollen, and the study of this, palynology, plays an important role in archaeology. Most pollen grains are very distinctive, like snowflakes, a fact which was recognised early in the 20th century. Most importantly, they are almost indestructible. Palynologists devised a series of "pollen zones" in which the climatic changes that happened at the end of the Ice Age were marked by the appearance of particular types of vegetation. Very broad chronological bands could be defined on the basis of the presence or absence of certain plants. It is not, however, unanimously accepted that pollen zones are universal in the western hemisphere. In the more recent past, local fluctuations in plant cover have reflected climatic changes, and cores are taken from peat bogs to trace the widespread occurrence of weeds of cultivation or periods of encroachment of wild plants on former areas of cultivation.

• Phytoliths, minute pieces of silica from the cells of plants, often survive when the rest of the plant has decayed. The drawback is that, although they survive well in large numbers, they are not readily attributable to particular plant species.

• Diatom analysis is used for the microscopic examination of plant remains. Diatoms are single celled algae with silica walls that survive long after the algae die. They are, like pollen, abundant and readily identifiable, but they are found in water sediments. It is possible to trace the variations in the nutrients in the water, which may be changed by such phenomena as agriculture or forest clearance in the vicinity of the lakes in which they are found.

• Larger plant remains survive on archaeological sites. In some cases plant impressions are found on pots, or were used as temper in the clay. Occasionally they are found as impressions on plaster or in the corrosion products on metal. Burnt grain (sometimes charred to prevent it germinating and then stored in pits) or charcoal from hearths of burned buildings can show how wood was used rather than the general plant cover in the neighbourhood. Plant remains can be found in the stomachs of mummies, faeces, or inside pots. In waterlogged deposits, frozen or extremely arid conditions organic material can survive well.

Fig.69. The impression of a fern on the base of a Roman pot.

(b) Bones and shells

These can provide a wealth of information about animals; soft tissue rarely survives, but bones, and particularly teeth, have a particularly high survival value. Some vertebrates are difficult to distinguish from one another - sheep and goats are very similar, for example, though the horn cores help to separate them. The analysis of the material involves identifying each bone (where this is possible - small fragments are often not identifiable) and producing an NISP ("number of identified specimens").

More significant however is the MNI ("minimum number of individuals") for each species, though this can be problematic unless very large bone assemblages are available for study. Bones can sometimes be sexed by size, and age at the time of death can be worked out from such things as the ossification of bone structures, wear on teeth, and tooth eruption. Most bones on sites come from domesticated animals, and a study of these can indicate diseases, when they were slaughtered, or the practices involved in butchery. If only some bones are present and not others, it suggests that ready butchered meat was brought in from outside. Favourite cuts can be inferred, and in the case of wild animal bones, evidence about hunting can sometimes be available.

Wild species provide information about the environment in the vicinity of the site, and gnawing marks on bones suggest the work of scavengers such as dogs. Other questions to which bones may provide answers concern whether animals such as horses were used for riding, draught or food (or possibly all three).

The bones of very small animals such as rats, mice, birds or fish can be difficult to see, but the same techniques of flotation used for plants can recover them. Fish bones are particularly elusive, and do not survive well. Sometimes, however, otoliths ("ear stones") and the spines of catfish survive, and under the microscope annual growth rings help study fishing patterns.

Marine shells were collected for food - in the Roman period for instance, oysters and other shellfish were traded many miles from their place of origin. Shells were sometimes used as tools.

Land molluscs are very informative about the environment, since certain types of snails prefer different environments such as grassland, woodland, shaded areas and so on. Climatic changes are also reflected in the type of snails found at different periods.

Insect remains such as pupae and beetle wing cases often survive. Blow-fly pupae have been used to prove bodies were left out in the open during decomposition. Insects are very sensitive to climatic change, so a study of insect types at different times on sites can be used to monitor climatic change.

Fig.70. Footprint of a small, cloven-hoofed animal on a Roman tile from Barton-in-Fabis, Notts, in 2001 from the trench shown in Fig.41. A second tile showed a similar imprint with that of a large dog, giving rise to much speculation about a chase before the tiles were fired.

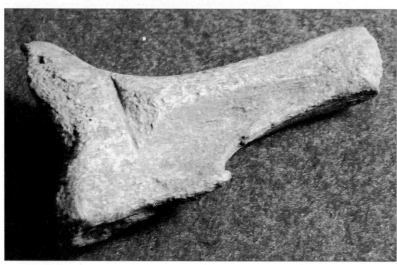

Fig.71. Bone with butchery cut, from the 6th century AD fort at Mote of Mark, Kirkcudbright.

4. Underwater archaeology can include wrecks, sites covered or lost through coastal erosion or cliff slide and lake deposits. Along with wetland studies, underwater archaeology requires very different techniques. It is appreciated that underwater sites should be excavated and recorded as meticulously as those on land, and the British-based Nautical Archaeology Society issues codes of conduct. Spoil (waste material in which finds may be contained) is removed using an air lift.

Prospecting techniques include magnetometry, which has proved very successful in locating wrecks. Underwater "excavation" requires specialist technology. In the 15th century, attempts were made in Lake Nemi near Rome to investigate two huge Roman ships that were part of local legend. In the following century divers were brought in from Genoa to investigate, using a diving bell with crystal window, and experiments were made with a diving suit. Very cumbersome diving suits were developed in the 19th century. It was not until 1928 that the Nemi wrecks were properly recorded: Mussolini drained the water in 1931 to reveal two small Roman vessels. Much information about Roman shipbuilding emerged from this early exercise, but in 1944, retreating troops set fire to the ships and the museum.

The commercial development of the aqualung in 1946 allowed divers to move around freely, but professional recording of underwater sites was slow to develop. In 1950, the Italian archaeologist Lamboglia watched helplessly as hundreds of Roman amphorae were destroyed by a salvage company that had offered its services free. He subsequently described the exercise as a "massacre of amphorae". This was the first recorded attempt by an archaeologist to recover information (not just treasure) from the seabed. The 1950s saw the "amphora rush" as amateur enthusiasts dived in the Mediterranean looking for wrecks. Around 1958, a metal grid was developed to facilitate better recording of finds.

Underwater archaeology is also concerned with submerged settlements, ranging from the remains of Alexandria off the Egyptian coast to Iron Age lake dwellings in Scottish lochs.

5. Theoretical archaeology. For periods where there are few or no written records archaeological material is classified according to theoretical models, many of which are derived from historical, socio-economic or political models (the Three Age System of Stone, Bronze and Iron Ages is a good example). These originated in hypotheses, many of which have had to be rethought as information and data retrieval has improved.

Although it remains the most valid method of handling such material, theory is not infallible. For instance, when the same principles were applied to historical periods, patterns were created that were nonsense in historical terms. Theoretical archaeology has gained popularity amongst academics rather than the general public, in particular in the last thirty years. Its advantage is that it is constantly updatable, but its disadvantage is that it is easily misunderstood and can be misleading if the hypothesis used is formed from unsound reasoning or insufficient or inaccurate data.

(a) "New (Processual) Archaeology"
In the 1960s there was a shake-up in the way people viewed archaeological evidence, mostly as an attempt to counter what was seen as the inaccuracy of the legacy from the antiquaries and others. In the USA, archaeology was much more closely tied to anthropology, since surviving native cultures could be studied and used to project back interpretations of the archaeological evidence for their ancestors. In 1968, David Clarke published **Analytical Archaeology** which advocated a similar approach to that of American theoretical pioneers such as Lewis Binford and Gordon Willey. This view of archaeology became known as "New" or "Processual" Archaeology.

In essence, "New Archaeology" argued that "Old Archaeology" collected data in the field, studied it in the laboratory, and then made inferences dictated by possibility. Clarke preferred to form hypotheses first and then looked at the whole spectrum of archaeological data before singling out a situation where a hypothesis might be tested to find out if it was correct.

A potential danger in this method is that any hypothesis will inevitably be based on assumptions and subconscious attitudes of the hypothesiser (ie it is likely to be derived from exactly the same sources as the frameworks it seeks to upturn).

Nonetheless, "New Archaeology" devised a daunting dictionary of jargon - for example, the process of hypothesis testing was called formulating a "hypothetico-deductive-nomological" model. Such jargon, however, is so user unfriendly that it has created a certain elitism and given "New Archaeology" a reputation for excessive intellectual complexity.

(b) Post-Processual Archaeology
Some of the more extreme views of "New Archaeology" led in the 1980s to a modification - post-processual archaeology - in which the role of the individual was given greater place. The term "post-processual" is the equivalent of "post-modernist" in literature, but it has also been described as "interpretive archaeologies". In essence, post-processual archaeology rejects the idea of laws governing all societies. Instead, it sees each society as different, and requiring to be studied using a diversity of approaches. It argues that there can be no one view of a society, and that each person approaching it is

Fig.72. Vitrified stone in the rampart at the Dark Age fort at Mote of Mark, Kirkcudbright showing the impressions of the burnt-out timber posts.

equally entitled to an individual view of it. This is also termed the "hermeneutic" view of the past.

Post-processual archaeology is suspicious of the exclusively scientific approach, arguing that the data and test methods are already coloured by theoretical factors and thus cannot be purely objective. It also argues that people in the past were as subject to their own thoughts as they are today, and that the thinking of the individual produced a reaction between their thoughts, their physical surroundings and material culture. Post-processual archaeology often has strong political motivation, and has what is seen as (but is by no means exclusively), a neo-Marxist concern with social awareness - maintaining that archaeologists should use the past to provide insights into the present world.

6. Experimental archaeology. This type of investigation has taken place since the 19th century, when Pitt Rivers made and tested prehistoric digging implements and studied the weathering and silting in the ditches left open after his excavations. Sir John Evans experimented in the 1860s, making and testing stone tools, with results that are still accepted.

Not all experiments have been happy. In 19th century Dublin, Dr. Robin Ball tried to find out how Bronze Age side-blown Irish horns worked, and as a result created (in the words of a contemporaneous account) "a deep bass note, resembling the bellowing of a bull. And it is a melancholy fact that the loss of this gentleman's life was occasioned by a subsequent experiment of the same kind. In the act of attempting to produce a distinct sound on a large trumpet....he burst a blood-vessel, and died a few days after".

In 1937, an experiment was carried out to see how the "vitrified forts" of Scotland might have been produced. These Iron Age sites have ramparts made of a mass of fused basalts, with impressions of timbers within them.

A section of timber-laced rampart, 4m long, 2m wide, and 2m high was built at a Stirlingshire colliery. The timber frame weighed 1.25 tons, and the rubble used to infill it, 7.5 tons. It was fired using 4 tons of heaped brushwood. Despite a 20 mph snowstorm, after three hours the outer face collapsed, followed by the inner. After five hours, the rubble was red hot, and the rampart smouldered for 20 hours. The cooled remains were excavated, when it was found the stone had melted into a solid mass at

Fig.73. Rebuilding the past with look-alike materials - the Roman fort at Cardiff rebuilt as Cardiff castle in the 19th century. The Roman wall remains can be seen at the bottom of the rebuild.

the base of the pile, and imprints of some of the timbers were left in the rock. It was calculated that a minimum temperature of 800 degrees C must have been achieved, or more probably as much as 1200 degrees C. At Butser, an experimental Iron Age farm now has newly built prehistoric houses, enclosures and grain storage in pits. Experiments with prehistoric farming methods include growing prehistoric crops and breeding "Iron Age" animals.

7. Conservation and reconstructing the past.

With the accepted need to preserve and conserve as much of the past as possible, emphasis has focussed on reconstruction of both sites and events. Few ancient buildings have survived intact and remains are often reduced to the footings of walls. Visitors therefore have difficulty in forming an impression of the original appearance of the structures. Further-

more, once the remains have been exposed they have to be conserved and protected to prevent further decay. There have been vigorous debates about whether it is right to "freeze" the appearance of the remains at such random points.

Accordingly, one viewpoint favours reconstructing the original appearance of a building, or part of it, to show what it would have looked like. The simplest form of reconstruction involves simply re-erecting fallen columns or arches and replacing fallen stones (as has happened at Stonehenge page 82). This policy was once followed on a number of castles and other monuments in state care by the Ministry of Works, who often used an "inch back" policy of showing what was rebuilt by setting the rebuilt part an inch back from the original wall face. Another device used on "restored" buildings was to mark the top of the original wall with a line of differently-coloured stone or

Fig.74. South Shields - reconstruction of a Roman gateway.

79

*Fig.75. Rebuilding the past from fallen pieces -
the library of Celsus, Ephesus in 1981.*

brick. In the case of Cardiff Castle, a Roman fort rebuilt by the Marquess of Bute in the 19th century, only the lower parts of the present walls are Roman.

Many of the apparently standing remains to be seen in the Mediterranean have been "rebuilt" in this way using the original stones. The classic example of this is at Ephesus in Turkey, where the Austrians have been excavating since 1895, initially using what is termed "anastylosis" (the re-erection of fallen columns). With 1.5 million visitors a year Ephesus is one of the most-visited archaeological sites in the world, and since 1954 an active programme of reconstruction has been underway. Since 80% of the stones from the façade of the Library of Celsus survived, they were used between 1973 and 1978 to reconstruct it.

After he excavated the Minoan palace of Knossos in Crete (claimed as the original Labyrinth in Greek myth) Sir Arthur Evans decided to rebuild parts of it, using concrete replacements for lost timber columns, which were then painted. Although Evans' reconstruction of Knossos has delighted generations of visitors and inspired interest in the past, it has come in for much criticism from those who feel it is inaccurate or misleading.

More recently, it has become fashionable to build replicas of buildings to help visitors understand what was once standing on the site or nearby. When these are rebuilt in the way it is believed they were originally put up, valuable insights can be gained without damage to ancient sites. Good examples of rebuilding in this way include the section of Hadrian's Wall rebuilt by schoolchildren at Vindolanda (Chesterholm), the prehistoric houses at Butser, Hants, which were built as part of a wider experiment (see page 79) or the Anglo-Saxon houses rebuilt at West Stow, Suffolk.

More ambitious rebuildings include a Roman gate at South Shields Roman fort (Fig.74.) and the Rose Theatre of Shakespeare's time in London.

Recreating the past by re-enacting activities or events has long been popular and will undoubtedly continue to be so.

Fig.76. Rebuilding the past in concrete -
Palace of Minos, Knossos, Crete in 1973.

Fig.77. Rebuilding the past with look-alike materials -
the Saxon village of West Stow, Suffolk.

Was Stonehenge always like that?

In the 19th century people could hire a hammer in Amesbury to chip a souvenir from Stonehenge. On the last evening of the 19th century one of the uprights of the sarsen circle fell with its lintel. In September 1901 the leaning upright of the biggest trilithon was straightened, having been slipping on to the bluestone in front of it since the 16th century. Reconstruction began in 1919 when four stones in the outer circle were straightened and stabilised (prior to this they were held up by steel and timber props). In 1958 more fallen stones were re-erected.

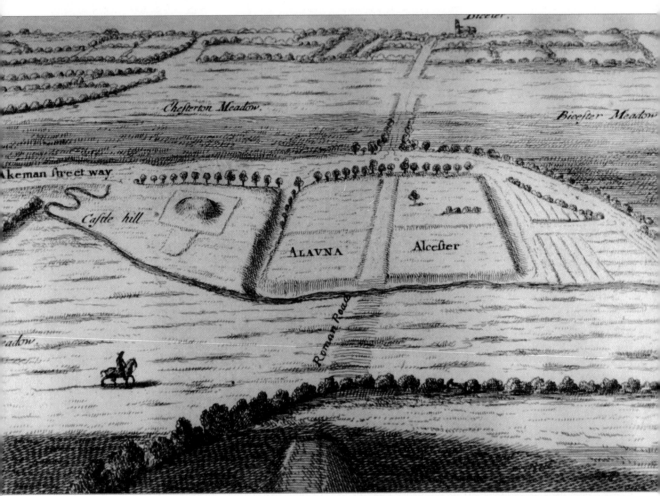

Fig.78. Interpreting the landscape - tracing a Roman road and medieval motte and field systems at Alcester, recorded by William Stukeley in the 18th century.

8. Landscape studies By and large landscape studies are non-destructive, and have the advantage of being accessible to amateurs. The study is closely allied to historical geography, geology and geography. This aspect of studying the past is particularly rewarding since each year new sites are discovered simply because local people notice changes in crop marks, or shadows. The author has spent years inadvertently observing field systems under different conditions and in different areas simply through various school runs which take place when shadows are long.

What are those bumps in that field?

Fig.79. Medieval field systems showing as ridges and furrows at Heronbridge, Cheshire in 1984.

Many human activities leave traces that are detectable from ground level or the air - much agricultural or building activity can be discerned thousands of years after the event - often as bumps and hollows in otherwise flat terrain.

Even the demolition of stone or timber buildings can leave traces.

The diversity can be illustrated by a few examples from Britain.

- Round bumps may be Bronze Age barrows (burial mounds) or, if very large, medieval mottes (mounds) on which timber castles stood.

- Long, substantial mounds may be Neolithic long barrows.

- Long banks and ditches may be traces of medieval ridge and furrow cultivation, which created low inverted-S shape bands in fields, with a low bank (the head rig) at the top.

- Long substantial banks may be the remains of linear boundaries marking off territories, though sometimes banks and ditches are found demarcating medieval and latter parish boundaries.

- Deserted medieval villages (DMVs) are often visible as sunken roadways with raised platforms on either side where the houses stood.

Fig.80. Interpreting the landscape - a disused gypsum mine can be seen snaking up the hill under shrubs at Barton-in-Fabis, Nottinghamshire.

● Banks and ditches enclosing rectilinear areas can be (amongst other things) Roman marching camps, Roman forts or medieval moated manors.

● In general terms, villages or houses before the medieval period tend to leave few surface indications, and the same thing applies to pre-Christian cemeteries (and some Christian) where tombstones were not erected.

● Rectangular hollows or bumps about a yard wide can be the remains of early archaeological trenching.

Fig.81. Sunken street and raised house platforms in the deserted medieval village of Wharram Percy, Yorkshire in 2003.

Fig.82. Deserted medieval village, deserted medieval church, and mill pond at Wharram Percy, Yorkshire in 2003.

Fig.83. 1950s Wheeler style trenches at Heronbridge Cheshire visible in 1985.

Who built it?

This question is closely related to "When and why was it built?" General deductions may be made by the process of elimination. There are no buildings standing above ground in Britain earlier than the Roman period (excluding standing stones, burial mounds, the few prehistoric stone-built dwellings of the Northern Isles and Cornwall, the Iron Age broch towers of northern Scotland and the earthworks of Iron Age forts).

For buildings below ground the shapes are important - a Roman fort was a very different shape from an Elizabethan manor house or a Celtic monastery, though sometimes the remains may be difficult to interpret, despite this.

Further deductions may be made by architectural comparison for which many textbooks and guidebooks exist.

● From Roman Britain the outer walls of some late forts have survived reasonably well such as: Richborough, Portchester and Burgh Castle; the walls of some towns, such as Caerwent, Silchester and Chester; the town gates of Lincoln and Colchester (the Balkerne Gate); and the lower parts of a number of other buildings. No buildings survive to roof height from Roman Britain.

Fig.84. Still standing - small standing stones on Bute, in 1997.

Fig.85. The Newport arch, as it was in the 19th century.

● In the Dark Ages secular building was all in timber until very late in the period, and the only surviving buildings are stone-built churches, though part of one late Saxon timber church survives at Greensted in Essex. There are about 400-500 churches in England with some Anglo-Saxon work in them. There are surviving timber-framed and stone-built buildings from the Middle Ages, which range from cathedrals through churches to tiny chapels, and from complex castles through fortified manor houses to the homes of town burgesses. Some town walls and gates survive.

● The earliest surviving stone-built domestic housing appears to date from the 12th century. From the 11th century only a few castles survive, notably the Tower of London and the Keep at Colchester (now a museum).

● For standing buildings the most definitive features are windows, doors and stonework. When studying surviving buildings, the approach is similar to that taken with below ground features - it is a question of working out the "layers" of building work and their sequence. Different types of masonry point to later re-building or repairs, tusking (projecting stones on a wall), or gable lines (a line of cement following the line of a former roof) point to parts of the building that were there once but have been demolished.

Fig.86. An Anglo-Saxon church tower, Lincoln with distinctive windows.

Blocked up windows or doors, or those in a later style, are often visible in the original walls.

Why was it built?

Buildings fall into a few main categories - **domestic** (including houses and animal shelters); **defensive** (forts, defended homesteads or military encampments); or **religious** (temples, churches or sanctuaries). Often they are grouped together and interrelated. Sometimes a site will have remains from many periods, especially if it enjoys benefits such as access by river or road, or good soils and climate.

Determining the function of a site or building is usually a combination of many lines of inquiry, beginning with field observation, artefacts and historical sources if available. Shape and the provision of internal or external features provide general information.

What is a DMV?

This term refers to "deserted medieval villages". In England this was originally thought to be the result of the Black Death (in 1349), when it was estimated that between a third and a half of the population died. More recent work has shown that there were many factors behind village desertion, including the increase in rainfall in the 13th century with the flooding of some sites, the changeover to sheep farming in the later Middle Ages (English wool was in big demand abroad), and the deliberate depopulation and relocation of people in the 18th century to enable parks to be built around stately homes.

What is a nucleated settlement?

This term is used to describe a cluster of houses, farms and other buildings that might be described in modern terms as a village or hamlet. The term is used to distinguish this type of occupation from dispersed, linear or ribbon development, where a community can be made up of a series of farms built along a road or scattered on a hillside.

Chapter 6

People

What did they look like?

Art can sometimes give an indication of the appearance of individuals. Sculptures for example may closely resemble depictions on coins that refer to a particular emperor, king or historic person. In the absence of such data, appearance can be reconstructed using forensic science to build up likenesses on the casts of skulls. This branch of archaeology developed out of the science of reconstructing facial features for murder victims being investigated by the police. Subsequently, using casts of skulls forensic artists have rebuilt the appearance of (probably) Philip of Macedon, King Midas, various mummies and bog burials, and some anonymous Britons (prehistoric, Roman, Anglo-Saxon and medieval).

The most dramatic reconstruction of this type was of the putative head of Philip of Macedon, father of Alexander the Great. What were believed to be three royal tombs were found at Vergina in Macedon, in 1977. The second tomb was intact but apparently finished in haste with a fresco and containing an assortment of treasures including silverware, and armour. The tomb was in two parts, each one with a marble sarcophagus containing a gold box with the starburst symbol of the royal Macedonian family that in turn contained a cremation wrapped in cloth. The bones in the gold box in the main chamber were of a man who had died between 35 and 55, and by a process of elimination (from historical sources) it seemed probable that they were those of Philip. Because the body had been cremated, some bones (including the skull), were very distorted but it was possible to create a restored version of the skull.

There was evidence of an injury which had cut the soft tissue to the bone and which would have lacerated an eyeball causing collapse and atrophy. It is known that Philip of Macedon was injured by an arrow in his eye at the battle of Methone, and it is also known he walked with a limp from war injuries. In the outer chamber at Vergina, greaves (leg armour) were found, which had been made to fit a man with one leg shorter than the other, though the bones showed no obvious injury.

What clothes did they wear?

Fig.87. Fresco painters from a Roman relief from Sens, France, a lively scene that shows not only clothing but work in progress.

Fig.88. Cupids dressed as gladiators, from a Roman mosaic at Bignor, Sussex.

Details of dress and personal belongings can also be seen from paintings, sculpture or manuscripts. Clothes rarely survive in British excavations, though leather and small pieces of cloth may sometimes be found in waterlogged conditions. In addition, impressions of cloth may be preserved in the corrosion products on brooches, from which the type of weaves can be studied. The position of buckles, pins, and other dress fastenings in graves can point to particular sartorial habits. Very occasionally more substantial items of clothing are preserved in peat bogs. Outside Britain, clothes survive rather better in the very dry climates of Egypt or Peru, and in frozen tombs in Siberia.

The most useful source for clothing comes from sculpture and wall paintings where these survive, though sometimes these are stylised and possibly even deliberate anachronisms.

What did they eat?

This question can sometimes be answered from food refuse, bones and microscopic plant remains. Sometimes impressions of seeds or plants were made on the clay of pottery before it was fired. Cooking utensils and very occasionally traces of food or drink have been found. A late Neolithic beaker from Ash-grove, Fife, probably contained mead, and some medieval cooking pots appear to have contained mutton stew. Another source of information about diet comes from cess pits - some food materials, such as tomato skins, are remarkably resilient. Much has been learned about diet from medieval sewage pits,

and eggs of parasitic worms have shown that round-worm and whip worm were endemic. One pit in Cuckoo Lane, Southampton (where documentary sources record a merchant called Richard of South-wick), produced the remains of grapes, figs, raspberries, strawberries, sloes, cherries, plums, wal-nuts and hazelnuts, as well as an assortment of other items including Iranian silk, Venetian glass and the skeleton of a Barbary ape. Cess pits from medieval urban sites have shown that herbs and spices were common, as were various fruits, especially figs, which appear to have been cheap.

What happened to the dead?

Fig.89. A Saxon skeleton during excavation at Sedgeford, Norfolk.

Some of the dead were buried, some were cre-mated, and some were thrown in rivers. It is also possible that some were exposed to the elements/ wildlife or even eaten, although there is little evi-dence of this. Some periods in the past (for example, the Iron Age) have left very little evidence for death and burial, although it is possible that the marked build up of ground under existing churchyards in Britain denotes pre-Christian burials. Burials in ditches where decomposition would quickly take place would also leave few traces.

Some burials show evidence of ritual or ceremony and grave goods. There is evidence from pagan Anglo-Saxon burials of people being buried with their horses, and from Viking burials of slaves or wives to accompany their deceased menfolk, as at Ballateare on the Isle of Man. Although it has been disputed, it has been suggested that an Anglo-Saxon female body at Sewerby in Yorkshire had been delib-erately buried alive.

Has archaeology uncovered evidence

of violent death?

From time to time archaeology produces evidence of death caused by battle, accidents, human sacrifice, executions and - in a few instances - murder.

• One of the earliest victims of a violent death through human agency known to archaeology was an Upper Palaeolithic child from Grimaldi in Italy, whose life was ended by an arrow in the backbone.

• Of slightly more recent date, at Fengate, Peterborough, four Neolithic bodies were found together in 1975 in an unmarked grave - an adult male and female aged about 25-30, a child aged about 8-12, and an infant of about 3-4. The man had a flint arrowhead lodged between the eighth and ninth ribs and it has been suggested that this was a family who had been the victims of an assassination.

More evidence for violent death comes from Roman Britain.

• A man with a Roman ballista bolt in his spine was buried at the Iron Age fort of Maiden Castle, Dorset, he is thought to have died defending the stronghold against the Romans.

• There is evidence for a murder from the civilian settlement outside the fort of Housesteads on Hadrian's Wall, where two bodies had been concealed under a newly-laid floor, one with a sword point stuck in it.

• At Dunstable, in a Roman cemetery, a second body was concealed in a previously dug grave (however, at other periods pushing half decaying remains into any available coffin was a fairly common contingency measure taken by over-worked sextons in overcrowded burial grounds and does not always imply murder).

• A murder victim was found with a knife protruding from his ribs during the excavation of a Roman bridge at Aldwickle, Northants.

• A female with 6th century belongings was found in a Roman well at Poulton Down, Wilts, 23ft down. She had fallen on a rock and had stones thrown on top of her, but to judge by the bloodstains on her skull, she had already met a violent end.

Is there evidence for violence

in Dark Age and Viking Britain?

• Excavations of the 7th century Anglo-Saxon royal cemetery at Sutton Hoo (Suffolk) uncovered in Mound 5 the cremated remains of a young man whose skull had been cut at least nine times by a sword or similar weapon.

• A succession of burials at Sutton Hoo contained bodies of people who had been hanged, beheaded or mutilated. These burials belonged to the period from the 7th to the 11th centuries, and some seem to have been interred around a large post, interpreted as a gallows, and perhaps a place of

public execution of the type known from history.

• Another Anglo-Saxon burial, from Eccles in Kent, had non-fatal perimortem injuries to the skull followed by three posterior cranial decapitating blows, preceded, it has been suggested, by a blade through the left eye. The victim, by that time dead, had his side opened by the slashing of the ribs and a blade thrust into the spine. The pathologist commented dryly that the incision was "not of surgical precision or motivation". It has been suggested that the assailant was a psychopath.

What about war victims?

Victims of war are fairly common.

● In the Iron Age fort at Sutton Walls (Hereford), decapitated skulls were found with cleanly severed vertebrae. These may have been connected with Celtic head-hunting, their heads used to adorn the fort gateway (a practice for which there is independent evidence).

● A number of war cemeteries have been excavated, perhaps the most dramatic being that at Little Big Horn, Montana, where General Custer took his last stand against the Sioux in 1876. One of the soldiers, aged about 25, had been shot in the chest by a .44 bullet, then shot in the head with a Colt revolver, and finally had his skull crushed with a Native American club.

● A war cemetery relating to the English Wars of the Roses. At Towton, Yorkshire, the victims of a battle fought in 1461 were dug up in 1996.

Is there evidence for human sacrifice?

Sacrifice, usually a part of widespread religious belief, is well documented in archaeology as well as history, though there is sometimes room for doubt about the motivation. The most famous examples are perhaps the Iron Age bog bodies, such as Tollund Man from Denmark or Lindow Man from Cheshire.

● Lindow Man was an outstandingly well-preserved body found in 1984 in a peat bog 10 miles from Manchester. He had been well-built, in his mid-20s and very fit apart from mild arthritis in the lower spine and some trouble with worms. After a last meal of a griddle cake, wearing nothing except a fox fur arm band, he was twice hit on the head with a blunt implement, was garrotted and had his throat cut (the exact order of these misfortunes is in doubt). A broken rib may have been caused by pressure from the knee of one of the men applying the garrotte. The body was thrown into a pool, probably during cold weather.

● The find was preceded in 1983 by the discovery of so-called "Lindow Woman", a skull with the hair, some tissue and part of the left eye still surviving. This was originally suspected of being a modern murder victim - a prisoner confessed to the police that he had killed his wife and buried her in his garden next to the peat bog, and thought that somehow her skull had become misplaced. Archaeologists proved him wrong. Whether or not he had murdered his wife, the skull belonged to a person who had died around the time of the Roman conquest of Britain.

● The servants who drank poison at Ur, a Sumerian city now in Iraq were almost certainly sacrificial victims (though other more imaginative explanations may be suggested). Around 74 people were buried in the king's tomb (known as the "death pit") circa 2,500 BC. They comprised members of the court, servants, soldiers, and musicians with harps, cymbals and systra (rattles). There were also four-wheeled wagons with their drivers and harnessed animals. All the victims were provided with little cups of poison or narcotic. It appears that the final act was when the executioners returned to arrange the drugged or dead bodies, kill the animals and leave the death pit for the earth to be poured in.

How many people were there?

Population estimates are notoriously difficult unless there is reliable documentary evidence such as the **Domesday Book**, Poll Tax returns or Census records. Archaeologists tend to make "guesstimates" based on the number of sites known at a given period, but it is almost impossible to tell if all settlements of a particular type were occupied simultaneously. It has been suggested that the entire population of the British Isles in the Upper Palaeolithic, at any one time, might not have been more than 250 people. In the Mesolithic it has been suggested that groups of people could have wandered the forests of Britain without ever meeting another group. By the Roman period the population had grown considerably - estimates range between 2 and 4 million.

What language did they speak?

Language leaves no trace in the archaeological record unless inscriptions are found, though clues are sometimes contained in place names as the changes in word-forms can sometimes be pinpointed from documentary evidence. It is possible that in time study of muscle attachments on skulls might indicate speech patterns. Even the existence of inscriptions need not imply that the general population spoke the language, or could read it. Coinage typically used inscriptions as well as images that conveyed news or propaganda about those in power. In some cases language can be very enduring but in others languages may be rapidly adopted, possibly a reflection of trade rather than political affiliations.

Do ancient people leave fingerprints or DNA?

Fingerprints have been found impressed on pots, on building daub or plaster, and even as chalky impressions on the antler picks in a Neolithic flint mine at Grimes Graves, Norfolk. Study of DNA and genetic printing are developing areas of archaeology, but attempts have been made in recent years to produce genetic maps of the British Isles through studying blood groups. The results have largely borne out what has been inferred about sites and artefacts. The genetic makeup of people in Wales is generally different to that in England. The same study suggests that the people of Shetland have close links with those in Scandinavia (through the Norse settlement), while in the central Lake District a similar link with Scandinavia is apparent. There is a distinct difference between the populations of Suffolk and Norfolk, perhaps reflecting the different homelands of Anglo-Saxon settlers. The most recent work has been concerned with the DNA mapping of Vikings - it has been argued that there is a very strong survival of Viking stock in the Wirral of Cheshire. Another study, although questioned, has argued that people living in the Cheddar Gorge of Somerset share DNA with Cheddar Man, a Palaeolithic burial.

A classic case of modern forensic archaeology solving ancient crimes is seen in the case of the assassination in 1918, of the Russian royal family. After prolonged research, in 1979 a burial pit was found in the woods outside Ekaterinburg, and identified as containing the remains of the massacred Romanovs. In 1991 the remains were archaeologically excavated and the bones studied in England, the USA and Russia. The DNA was matched with that of surviving relatives, including HRH the Duke of Edinburgh. The conclusion was that the bones were indeed those of the Romanovs, including the Grand Duchess Anastasia whose fate had been in doubt due to claims by the impostor Anna Anderson.

What was the role of women and children?

This topic has been of particular concern in archaeology in the last 20 years, reflecting contemporary interests, but evidence can be difficult both to obtain and to interpret. Some recent work has focussed upon the evidence provided by burial practice, where it has been seen that the simple explanation for grave goods is not necessarily the correct one. A few examples are taken here.

In pagan Anglo-Saxon cemeteries the presence of weapons does not necessarily mean that the person buried with them was a warrior. Men buried with female accoutrements are believed to have been priests connected with certain cults.

Certain types of artefact are associated with particular age bands. It is possible that key-like objects suspended from the waist in female burials are connected with childbirth, since they are not associated with burials of children or the very old.

Children's burials occasionally contain weapons that they could not have wielded, suggesting that such things were status symbols. Some of the "effigies" found from prehistoric contexts may have been toys.

Can individual people be identified

even if their names are not known?

Individuals can rarely be identified without inscription or written records - despite the circumstantial evidence it is not 100% certain that the remains found at Vergina were of Philip of Macedon (page 89). Sometimes through a process of elimination and inference, a name might be tentatively forwarded for a burial. It is believed for instance that the person buried in Mound 1 at Sutton Hoo was a king called Redwald, because the dates of the archaeological material and historical sources seem to fit; but there is no firm evidence for this identification.

Personal names are fairly frequently found on items such as pottery or jewellery. The Alfred Jewel, now in the Ashmolean Museum is inscribed in Latin "Alfred had me made" which has led to the theory that it was made on the order of Alfred the Great, but other such inscriptions may refer to the maker as much as the owner.

Fig.90. Inscription in a Roman mosaic at Bignor, Sussex, possibly the initials of the mosaicist.

Have any dramatic moments

been recorded by archaeology?

Archaeology is full of dramatic demonstrations of the reality of historical facts.

● When Sir Mortimer Wheeler excavated the Iron Age hillfort at Maiden Castle in Dorset, he found a war cemetery of those defending the fort against the Roman army led by the general Vespasian (later emperor).

● At Alesia in France excavations between 1860 and 1865 revealed the siege works thrown up by Julius Caesar around the Iron Age Celtic capital where the Gaulish leader Vercingetorix finally surrendered.

● At Masada, the remains have been found of the besieged population who took poison rather than be taken prisoner by the Romans after a ruthless two year siege.

How long did people live in the past?

Contemporary life expectancy is constantly extending, but statistics for the past are random and depend not only on discovery of cemeteries, but the systematic analysis of the remains, which has rarely been carried out. It is possible here to outline only a few examples.

In the period between the late 18th and early 19th century, females and males in the cemetery at Spitalfields, London who reached maturity, all seem to have died around the age of 56. Males and females were equally represented, but a third were juveniles.

In pagan Anglo-Saxon England life expectancy seems to have been around 45 years, but since it is difficult to determine ages after this age some skeletons may in fact represent older people.

Neanderthals seldom reached the age of 50, and most died in their 40s.

In the Roman cemetery at Cirencester, the average age at death for males was 40.8 years, the average for females 37.8 years, though members of both sexes sometimes reached 65 years.

Occasionally, inscriptions on tombstones indicate an age of over 100.

Are ancient diseases transmitted

from archaeological sites?

The most celebrated instances of this are the stories of curses of the pharaohs' tombs, which are as yet unproven. In other instances, however, it is known that diseases can remain dormant for many years, even centuries. Anthrax for example is known to survive 50 years or more. Protective clothing is advisable during excavation of certain sites and tetanus protection imperative.

Can diseases and injuries be detected archaeologically?

Diseases that affect soft tissue can rarely be detected archaeologically, unless bodies are preserved through mummification, very dry, very wet, or frozen conditions.

• Accidents often leave very obvious evidence, not only for violent death, but injuries. A Neanderthal man from the cave at Shanidar in Iraq had lived to the age of about 40, despite having been partially blinded by a blow to his left eye, he had a fractured foot, arthritis in knee and ankle, and a withered left arm as a result of an injury in childhood. As he would not have been fully functioning in a food-gathering society, he must have been cared for by others.

• There is some evidence for the deliberate mutilation of skulls by binding. This is apparent from skulls of people living in Eastern Europe under Hunnic domination in the 5th century AD.

• Archaeology has also produced evidence for scalping, done just prior to burial, on pre-Columbian Indian skulls.

• Many diseases leave traces on bones. Polio was detected in a 4,000 year old burial of a girl aged about 20 from the United Arab Emirates.

• A Roman from Baldock, Essex, had lower leg fractures with an open wound that had allowed infection to attack the bone. The pitting to the leg bone showed that osteomyelitis had set in. A further wound to the lower leg resulted in a pus-discharging and (presumably), evil-smelling sore.

• A similar problem seems to have affected the "Prince of Stonehenge" (the occupant of a rich Beaker burial). He, too, must have been extremely unpleasant to be near, though he seems to have survived for a considerable time after injury.

• Congenital deformity often leaves obvious traces. A mummified female foetus from Tutankhamen's tomb in Egypt displayed Sprengel's deformity, that had resulted in spina bifida and one shoulder higher than the other.

• Arthritis was very common in antiquity, as now. A Roman cemetery at Cirencester in Gloucestershire contained 450 skeletons of which about half the males showed signs of arthritis in most joints of the body. Several others showed spina bifida and other congenital defects of the spine.

• Bodies at a Roman cemetery at Poundbury, Dorset, contained a very high concentration of lead, possibly due to the use of lead eating utensils. This feature is also found in burials of some medieval monks where it may be attributable to pewter tableware.

• Tuberculosis first appeared before the fourth millennium BC in the Near East, where it was probably spread by the cattle of the first farmers, through droplets. In the Middle Ages it was transmitted rapidly through the dense population areas of the growing towns.

• Leprosy is known from a skeleton of the 4th century BC in Egypt. It increased throughout the period down to the 13th century AD, but then seems to have receded quite rapidly, ceasing to be an endemic disease in Britain by the 17th century. This decline was matched by an increase in tuberculosis; the two diseases are mutually exclusive and provide immunity against one another.

Were people shorter in the past?

It is sometimes suggested that people were shorter (ie to judge by the low doors in some old houses), but where evidence exists, it seems they were only a little shorter on average. Evidence from skeletons is difficult to evaluate, and there are added factors that would affect the height of individuals or groups, such as nutrition, shelter, exposure to disease, or harsh conditions in childhood. Simply because heights during the 20th century in the western world have increased does not necessarily imply they have been doing so uniformly throughout history. Heights probably fluctuated in different areas, under differing conditions. The average Roman woman in Cirencester was 5ft 2in, the average man 5ft 6.5in. The oldest dwarf in the world was a male who died aged about 17 in Italy in the tenth millennium BC. He was about 3ft 7in to 3ft 11in tall. The small suits of medieval armour often brought forward as evidence, and which can sometimes be seen in stately homes, are now thought to be the outgrown suits of youths.

Did people have surgical skills?

There is impressive evidence for ancient surgery, as well as surgical equipment, which is well-known from Roman and occasionally European Iron Age contexts.

Trepanning - the removal of a piece of bone from the skull - is a type of surgery often found in antiquity which may have been used for medical or for ritual purposes. Surprisingly, the wounds quite often seem to have healed over and the removed piece of bone in some cases kept until death presumably as a "souvenir".

A group of four 6th century adult skulls from Norfolk and one from Suffolk all seem to have been trepanned by the same skilled surgeon who has been named "the Master of the Gliding Gouge".

Other examples of surgery include the dismembered skeleton of a foetus from Poundbury, Dorset, which displayed cut marks in exactly the positions that Soranus, a Roman surgeon, recommended for removing a dead baby from the womb to save the mother.

Can you tell anything from teeth?

Palaeopathologists can make many deductions from teeth. Dental caries was comparatively rare in antiquity due to the dearth of sugar in the diet. The oldest evidence for a filling was in the tooth of a Nabataean buried about 2,000 years ago in Palestine. One of his teeth had been filled with copper wire, which might have caused major problems, since copper oxide is poisonous. Rudimentary false teeth are known from Egypt and the grit in the diet of medieval monks has been shown to produce attrition.

Chapter 7

Does it ever go wrong?

Archaeology is a constantly developing subject, which means that new discoveries change perceptions of the past. In addition, the evidence is sometimes misinterpreted. Scientific tests and analyses are often less accurate than might be expected and need to be treated with caution. Deductions and inferences when analysing data must also be subject to caution. Often a particular interpretation may be put forward in order to excite popular interest and therefore funding, for instance.

However, allowing for unavoidable human errors, there have been a number of hoaxes and major mistakes.

Have archaeologists ever been fooled by hoaxes?

Sometimes hoaxes are more than fleeting jokes by wags attempting to test a site director's knowledge.

A famous British fraud was (probably) perpetrated by Charles Dawson, a solicitor from Lewes in Sussex, who created Piltdown Man - which was seen as the "missing link" between apes and humans. In 1908, Dawson began investigating a quarry at Piltdown, asking the workmen to inform him of bones and flints they found. Allegedly in due course they produced a small piece of "brown coconut" that turned out to be a fragmentary parietal bone of a human skull. Soon, another piece turned up that fitted with it, and eventually assisted by a palaeontologist from the British Museum, Dawson "uncovered" a fine series of relics from a small hole, including flints, more human bones and some of extinct animals. The "human" was given the name of *Eoanthropus Dawsonii* (Dawson's Dawn Man) and was presented to the world in 1913.

Dawson died in 1916, and although some people were sceptical of Piltdown Man almost from the outset, it was not until 1953 that the relevant scientific tests were developed to disclose the hoax. These proved that the Piltdown jawbone was from a modern chimpanzee, with the teeth abraded and filled with mineral crystals. The skull was older - but probably only by about 600 years. It was suggested it had come from a medieval monk. Jawbone and skull had been stained to match, and the animal bones were found to have come from a variety of sites, not necessarily in Britain.

What forgeries have been made?

During the Renaissance, even Michelangelo produced a fake Roman sculpture and sold it as genuine.

The forgery of antiquities increased in the 18th century - a forger called Becker "invented" coins which he kept in a box on his coach so they were buffeted around and "aged". His forgeries passed into the collection of George III, and still occasionally turn up.

Forgery in the 20th century has been more difficult to detect, since forgers have gone to considerable length to counter the scientific tests that may be applied.

Fig.91. Forgery of a tetradrachm of Athens, in neater style than the original (Fig.92.).

Fig.92. Tetradrachm of Athens, struck in the late 5th century BC.

Can aerial photographs be wrong?

The photographs are unlikely to be wrong, but the interpretation of them may well be since features may be caused by quite different agencies than the apparent archaeological ones. Geological features can often resemble archaeological - for example jointing in limestone can produce a system of squares that resemble fields. Modern cultivation methods (such as square ploughing, differential manuring and crop spraying) the presence of systems of field drains, and even the evidence of crop trials can all confuse the unwary and lead to costly mistakes. Tramlines have been mistaken for double Roman ditches, walls for ditches, and ditches for walls, causing considerable distortion of the facts.

Can scientific analysis be wrong?

Scientific data may easily become distorted. The most common problem perhaps arises in radiocarbon dating, where the material selected has been contaminated by more recent carbon, such as cigarette ash. Analysis of metals produces distorted results if the surface alone has been sampled - the surface may have been "enriched" or the processes of corrosion can mean that some elements have been reduced or removed.

Do archaeologists change their minds about dates or other data?

Archaeologists are constantly reappraising data. As dating methods become more accurate, dates for sites and objects change. A casual survey of books published over the past 50 years would show that Stonehenge is apparently ageing at a rate far in excess of the years that are passing. The desire to prove history (or myth) true by archaeology has led to a number of interpretational errors, which emphasises the necessity of keeping an open mind, and for constant reappraisals of material as knowledge and technology advances. Interpretation of entire sites also changes in the light of new research or new insights.

● Heinrich Schliemann, the first excavator of Troy, set out to find the city described by Homer in the Illiad. Convinced the city must have been very grand, he dug through the insubstantial remains of the site now known as Troy VIIb, to expose remains that fitted his ideas of the hometown of Helen of Troy. A cache of jewels from this impressed him so much he had his wife photographed wearing what were thought to be the "jewels of Helen". In fact the remains of "Helen's" Troy were the levels he had dug through. Schliemann's obsession with Homer also led to him to believe at Mycenae in Greece he had "gazed on the face of [king] Agamemnon" when he found a burial with a gold face mask. Once again, his find was much older than the period of the Trojan War.

Fig.93. Antiquaries getting it wrong - a bucket mount interpreted as a crown from a Dark Age burial at Xanten, Germany (after Wright, 1854).

Fig.94. Antiquaries getting it wrong - the trench through the mound at Hissarlik, Turkey (Troy) that was dug by Schliemann who mistakenly dug through the Homeric city of Troy he was seeking.

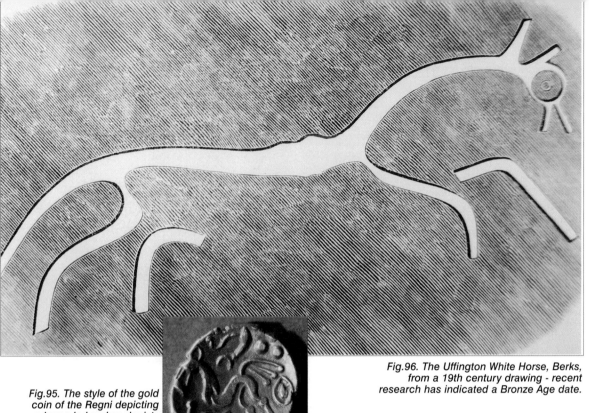

Fig.95. The style of the gold coin of the Regni depicting a horse led archaeologists to surmise the White Horse of Uffington dated from the Iron Age (but see Fig.96.).

Fig.96. The Uffington White Horse, Berks, from a 19th century drawing - recent research has indicated a Bronze Age date.

• In the 19th century, in particular, people found it difficult to accept that "barbarian" people could have produced fine works of art. The art treasures of the Iron Age Celts were long believed to have been Roman, and the excavator of Anglo-Saxon burial mounds, Bryan Faussett was convinced he was unearthing Roman jewels.

• When a timber post-built hall at Balbridie in Perthshire was excavated, it was assumed to be Dark Age. A sherd of Neolithic pottery in a posthole, however, alerted suspicion and subsequent radiocarbon dates from the site showed the site to be Neolithic (before 3500 BC).

Have valuable objects or important sites ever been lost and not recognised?

Perhaps the most famous is the first hoard of priceless Iron Age gold torcs (neck rings) from Snettisham (Norfolk). When ploughed up in 1948, the coppery-looking metal tubes were believed to be part of a brass bedstead, and a find the next day looked like "green string". They were thrown aside within sight of the busy main road. The find was reported in due course to the owner of the field who took expert advice.

Other finds have been discarded on discovery, including an amphora (wine storage jar) that came from a rich Iron Age burial at Welwyn Garden City. When a gas pipeline was being laid to a new estate, the workmen pulled out two amphorae, and saw a third. One of the sub-contractors took the amphorae home, intending to use them as garden ornaments, but left them in his garage until a friend saw them about two months later and suggested they might be ancient.

Chapter 8

The law and ethics

Archaeology, along with most other subjects, has not escaped heavy controversy concerning a variety of ethical and moral questions. The law has been amended and developed to reflect current thinking, though many areas of confusion and contention remain. Some of the most pressing concerns relate to the treatment of the dead and the balance between the need for society to progress with modern buildings and the wish to preserve archaeological material *in situ* for future generations. Some concerns are reflected in the current legal restrictions, but the question has been debated for decades; I once sat a university examination that included the mystifying question "What is the moral significance of a post-hole?"

Archaeology is destruction - is this true?

This phrase is generally used to bring attention to the fact that remains of the past are not renewable resources and should be respected. It refers to the fact that once investigated, the layers and features of an archaeological site can never be replaced. However, the rarely quoted corollary to the statement is the practice of all techniques of studying the past creates new knowledge and new perceptions. These in turn keep the subject alive and public interest high enough to care about the past including preserving as much as possible. Developments such as experimental archaeology and re-enactions of life in the past either through computers or in "play acting" are currently adding a dimension of creativity to the subject.

Conversely, leaving sites to the destructive results of farming methods, pesticides, natural erosion as often happens when a site is "protected" by legal restrictions can be highly destructive.

What is/was the Rescue Movement?

In the late 1960s in Britain, it was realised that archaeological sites were being destroyed at an ever-increasing rate due to development, road building, new farming methods (such as deep ploughing), and forestry plantation. The principle was established that all such sites should be professionally excavated before destruction, to establish basic facts such as date, extent, and preservation. The viewpoint is now embodied in policies of conservation, and the threats to sites are now seen to include pesticides and other chemicals, natural erosion and excavation itself. Recent legislation has crystallised official policies (see Valetta and EU legislation).

One drawback in this commendable policy is that only small areas of sites are routinely investigated, under restrictions of time and money, and investigations are dictated not by the sites themselves, but the potential. Any inferences made from such material are clearly of limited use and must be made with caution.

Furthermore, many artefacts and samples have been stored for many years, unprocessed. Inevitably such material stands in danger of becoming detached from its records, muddled and subject to mould or decay, so that rather than preserving material and information for the future we stand in danger of bequeathing a legacy of tedious, soul-destroying chores and incomplete records.

Is there a downside to "Rescue" policies?

Thirty years into the policy there has been an emphasis on the collection of data from threatened sites at the expense of wider research and reappraisal of material. It has become clear that many aspects of archaeological interpretation will stagnate at a point somewhere in the late 1960s or progressively become distorted as PhD theses (for example) deal with only random subjects. An unspecified number or sites currently masquerade under the wrong categorisation due to "historical accident" based on misunderstanding over ancient historical sources, possibly due to the emphasis on scientific based investigation.

To give an analogy: it would surely be advisable to ascertain that the books that our grandparents placed in the attic a century ago really are the great works of literature and reference they claimed (either because they believed it or because they had an undisclosed agenda), and not merely multiple, dog-eared copies of the same light Gothic romance. We stand in danger of collecting further copies of such novels and discarding works of great literature that do not measure up to the outmoded criteria.

What are "portable antiquities"?

Portable antiquities are any found objects that are not earth fast and do not constitute sites - usually small objects of stone, metal, glass or pottery. Metal detector finds come under this label. The law protects such objects - metal detecting is prohibited on scheduled sites, which are individually protected by law (monuments, for example), and objects found on them by chance must not be removed. In England and Wales on unscheduled sites chance discoveries of portable antiquities are as a general rule the property of the landowner, except where The Treasure Act applies.

In Scotland, a legal principle called Bona Vacantia applies, which means all antiquities found belong to the Crown, and must be reported to the police or local museum. The Procurator Fiscal then reports them to the Queen's and Lord Treasurer's Remembrancer, who puts them before a Treasure Trove committee that decides if they are Treasure Trove and where (ie to which museum) they should go. The finder may be compensated with the commercial value of the find. In Northern Ireland and in the Isle of Man a similar situation prevails (see also Treasure Act).

How many finds of "treasure" are reported each year?

A survey in 1995 calculated that at least 400,000 archaeological objects were discovered each year, and the great majority were unrecorded. Of this, treasure finds constituted about 5% of the total. When the laws of Treasure Trove were operating, about 25 cases were reported a year. This has increased tenfold to 250 a year. As a result, the British Museum currently employs a team of eight people full-time on treasure work.

Is there a black market in antiquities?

There is undoubtedly a major worldwide problem with illicit antiquities trading. However, Britain never was at the hub of a major civilisation so, although some important pieces of ancient art have been found over the years in British soil, richly-furnished tombs of the type frequently discovered in Mediterranean lands, Egypt, China or Latin America are not a feature of British archaeology.

The legal situation is clear: in Britain all antiquities of whatever value (excluding coins worth less than £35,000) require an export licence. Whether this is granted or not depends on the Waverley Criteria, set out by Lord Waverley in 1950:-

1. Is the object so connected with British history and national life that its departure would be a misfortune?

2. Is it of aesthetic value?

3. Is the object outstanding for the study of some branch of art and learning or history?

In point of fact, comparatively few licences are applied for and, once the object has left the country, it cannot be regained.

The active debate about the antiquities trade has led to Sotheby's closing down their antiquities deptartment in the UK, and institutions such as the Getty Museum putting time limits on the purchase of objects without a provenance. In 1970, Unesco held a convention on the Means of Prohibiting and Preventing the Illicit Import, Export and Transfer of Ownership of Cultural Property. America (but not the UK) agreed to follow this and to regard all unprovenanced objects purchased before 1973 to be licit and those purchased after that date to be illicit, unless shown otherwise.

What is the Treasure Act?

It was long felt that the laws of Treasure Trove were inadequate for defining ownership of antiquities. As a result, in 1997 the Treasure Act was introduced, which replaced Treasure Trove. The Treasure Act distinguished between coins and other objects, and got round the problem posed by the Snettisham find. It stated that all objects at least 300 years old containing 10% or more silver, and all associated finds (whatever they are made of), found in the same place or which had previously been together with another object in that treasure, have to be reported within 14 days of finding them or realising they might be treasure. In addition, all base metal finds that are prehistoric must, since January 2003, be reported. All coins from the same find (ie two or more) provided they are at least 300 years old must be reported, but if they contain less than 10% gold or silver there must be many of them.

What happens if gold or silver is found?

Until recently, in England and Wales, the main concern has been with Treasure Trove (items of gold and silver). The laws regarding Treasure Trove had their roots in the Middle Ages. For a find to be Treasure Trove it had to be the case that there is nobody around who has a strong legal claim to it and that the object or objects were buried with the intention of reclaiming them later. Thus, objects buried in graves belonged to the landowner, not the Crown (see Treasure Act).

What is gold or silver for legal purposes?

What constitutes gold or silver? Nine carat gold is only 37.5% gold, and many "silver" looking objects are mostly base metal. In a famous legal case it was claimed that a hoard of base silver Roman coins of the 3rd century found at Coleby, Lincs, contained almost no silver at all, and was therefore not Treasure Trove. The case went to the High Court, where it was concluded that since the people originally using the coins treated them as silver, they should be deemed to be Treasure Trove.

A hoard of Iron Age treasure found at Snettisham, Norfolk in a pit in 1990 was found to be a mixture of Treasure Trove and non-Treasure Trove. Roughly three-quarters of the objects were of precious metal, the rest of base metal with a precious metal content. So that the find could be kept together, in that instance the landowner gave the non-Treasure Trove finds to the nation.

What is the Portable Antiquities Scheme?

In 1997, in conjunction with the Treasure Act, the Portable Antiquities Scheme was launched to encourage the voluntary reporting of finds. By the end of March 2004 the Scheme had been extended to all parts of England and Wales employing 36 Finds Liaison Officers and a central unit.

During the period 1 April 2003 until 31 March 2004 over 47,000 archaeological objects had been recorded, nearly two thirds of this total having been discovered using a metal detector, the rest being found by other means.

The scheme's Website (www.finds.org.uk) allows public access to over 64,000 records and over 21,000 images.

What happens about dead people?

The ethics of excavating human remains are a serious issue. In England there was a tendency in the past to treat remains believed to have been of Christians with reasonable respect, but to treat the remains of "pagans" in a cavalier fashion. In England until comparatively recently, an Act of Parliament was needed to permit Christian cemeteries to be disturbed.

In Scotland the law is still quite clear and burials, Christian or pagan, must be left where they are, unless found by chance in circumstances where this is impossible. In Scotland, too, it is considered that human remains should be kept with or close to the objects that were buried with them. It is normal in Britain to re-bury Christian remains after they have been studied, usually in a local cemetery with a burial service.

The diversity of religions in contemporary Britain has heightened respect for all beliefs, including those no longer held by anyone. In the past, however, there have been serious problems in Australia and the USA with the lack of respect shown to Aborigine and Native American burial sites. There are clearly problems over what style of ceremony at reburial would be acceptable for remains of people whose religious beliefs cannot be ascertained.

How is archaeology regulated?

The main body responsible for archaeology in the UK is Central Government through English Heritage, Historic Scotland and Cadw (in Wales). Local Authorities have responsibility for developments that might threaten sites. There is much legislation including the Ancient Monuments Acts and, more recently the European Convention on the Protection of Archaeological Heritage. This was convened in 1969 and updated in 1992 at Valetta, Malta. Britain signed in March 2001. The legislation sets out some general rules for the protection of the archaeological heritage, to be applied in all the signatory countries - Austria, Belgium, Britain, Bulgaria, Cyprus, Denmark, France, Germany, Greece, Iceland, Italy, Liechtenstein, Luxembourg, Malta, Portugal, Spain, Sweden, Switzerland, USSR, Vatican and Yugoslavia.

The way the legislation is interpreted varies between countries.

At the time of writing it is permitted for excavations to take place with the consent of the landowner if the site is not subject to contrary legislation (ie is Scheduled, Guardianship or protected by other legislation). However, even on land that is not subject to any restriction, the excavation of a few cubic feet of excavated material for evaluation purposes may be held to be developing the land and held subject to Planning Permission under PPG 16. On Scheduled or Guardianship sites (which are deemed to be of national importance and thus subject to many restrictions) permission must be sought even for the use of geophysical equipment that does not enter the ground.

Who pays for archaeology?

Ultimately, the general public pays for the vast majority of archaeological work (and those employed in it) and is asked to accept road diversions and alternative building sites, or restrictions in land use in the name of preserving archaeological remains for the future. Grants are available from many Charitable Trusts, Local and Government agencies as well as directly from charges to participants so obtaining funding for any project is inevitably a lengthy and complex procedure. With archaeological studies growing increasingly more complex, the danger is that those paying will lose touch with what they are paying for. There is, however, a strong body of opinion that opposes any kind of popular involvement or spreading of information outside the profession (defined as those in permanent paid, primarily archaeological, employment).

Chapter 9

How can I get involved?

Britain is unusual in having a strong and well-respected tradition of amateur archaeology. In most areas professional archaeologists welcome public involvement and consider that the dissemination of information and experience is of prime importance.

Fig.97. Anglo-Saxon tablet weaving at Sedgeford, 2001.

What can I do - how can I get involved?

The Council for British Archaeology (CBA) have a useful website at www.britarch.ac.uk and can be contacted at Bowes Morrell House, 111, Walmgate, York, YO1 9WA.

By joining the CBA you become a member of the regional group in which you live, and get an information pack on joining, a bi-monthy magazine, *British Archaeology*, and information about excavations that take volunteers. Membership is currently £27 per annum.

A junior archaeologists' club run by the CBA is called The Young Archaeologist's Club (membership £7.50 per annum).

The Council for Independent Archaeology (www.independents.org.uk) exists to promote both amateur archaeology and independent archaeology in Britain - the subscription is currently £6 per annum or £20 for five years.

A subscription to *Current Archaeology* (9 Nassington Road, London NW3 2TX) will buy a bi-monthly magazine reporting on the latest discoveries and developments in Britain, and each year free to subscribers the *Archaeology Handbook* which lists digs, training courses, local societies, groups and other interested parties on a local basis. On a world-wide basis, *Current World Archaeology* was launched in 2003 to cover international developments.

WEA or local university Departments of Adult Education often run archaeology courses, sometimes in the case of the latter leading to Certificates or Diplomas.

How can I make a career in archaeology?

There are many routes in to this notoriously low-paid occupation. Due to the different specialist branches it is almost impossible to advise - clearly the qualifications will vary and it is best to obtain advice from the employing bodies themselves. There are A-level courses, degrees and diplomas in a wide variety of subjects including field archaeology, landscape studies, historical geography, museum studies, and heritage management. There are opportunities, once qualified, in field units, universities, museums and local and central government.

Since the subject is so diverse it is also possible for those with special preferences, disabilities, talents or ambitions to find a niche. Many holiday companies offer archaeological tours and some excavations offer hands-on experiences - these are often advertised in the archaeological magazines.

Fig.98. Most people's idea of what archaeology is all about - finding a hoard of coins. From J.Y. Akerman's "Coins of the Romans Relating to Britain", 1844.

Fig.99. The archaeological sites of the future? A sugar beet factory at Newark, Notts during floods.

What is the correct clothing for an archaeologist?

This is often the first question asked before a piece of fieldwork is undertaken. Obviously, the conditions on the day and the site must be the guide, and the project organisers should give you guidance. As in all archaeological work be prepared for the unexpected. To this end, I leave readers and would-be archaeologists with the following excellently open-minded advice.

Sir Flinders Petrie carried out his work in Egypt during the day wearing only his pink underwear, which in his own words "kept the tourist at bay, as the creature [Petrie] seemed to him too queer for inspection" (**Seventy Years in Archaeology**, 1931, 21). At night when he was able to work inside the Great Pyramid with greater ease due to the freedom from tourists, he said he dressed like "the Japanese carpenter who had nothing on but a pair of spectacles, except that I do not need the spectacles".

Notes

Bibliography

Aitken, M.J. (1990)	**Science-based Dating in Archaeology**, London.
Aston, M. & Rowley, T. (1984)	**Landscape Archaeology**, London.
Aston, M. (1997)	**Interpreting the Landscape: landscape archaeology and local history**, London.
Bagnall, R.S. (1995)	**Reading papyri, writing ancient history**, London.
Baillie, M.G. (1995)	**A slice through time: dendrochronology and precision dating**, London.
Barker, P.A. (1986)	**Understanding Archaeological Excavation**, London.
Barker, P. (1993)	**Techniques of Archaeological Excavation**, 3rd Ed., London.
Bass, G. (1966)	**Archaeology under Water**, London.
Bewley, B. (1996)	**Air Photography for Archaeology**, London.
Binford, L.R. (1972)	**An Archaeological Perspective**, New York.
Blot, J.Y. & Campbell, A. (1996)	**Underwater Archaeology. Exploring the World Beneath the Sea**, London.
Bowman, S. (1991)	**Radiocarbon Dating**, London.
Bowman, S. (Ed) (1991)	**Science and the Past**, London.
Brisbane, M. & Wood, J. (1996)	**A future for our past? An introduction to Heritage Studies**, London.
Brothwell, D.R & Higgs, E. (Eds)	**Science in archaeology**, London.
Brown, A. (1987)	**Fieldwork for Archaeologists and Local Historians**, London.
Chamberlain, A.T. (1994)	**Human Remains**, London.
Clark, A. (1990)	**Seeing beneath the Soil. Prospecting methods in archaeology**, London.
Daniel, G. (1975)	**A Hundred and Fifty Years of Archaeology**, London.
Dowman, E.A. (1970)	**Conservation in Field Archaeology**, London.
Ceram, C.W. (1952)	**Gods, Graves and Scholars, The Story of Archaeology**, London.
Chamberlain, A.T.	**Interpreting the past: human remains**, London.
Clarke, D.L. (1968)	**Analytical Archaeology**, London.
Coles, J. (1979)	**Experimental Archaeology**, London.

Coles, J. (2001)	**Digging Up the Past**, London.
Deuel, L. (1969)	**Flights into Yesterday**, London.
Greene, K. (2003)	**Archaeology: an Introduction**, rev. ed., London.
Harris, E.C. (1989)	**Principles of archaeological stratigraphy**, London.
Henderson, J. (2000)	**Science and the Archaeology of Materials: an investigation of inorganic materials**, London.
Hunter, J. & Ralston, I. (1993)	**Archaeological Resource Management in the UK**, Stroud.
Jones, B.	**Past imperfect: the story of rescue archaeology**, London.
Lowenthal, D. (1985)	**The Past is a Foreign Country**, Cambridge.
Mays, S. (1998)	**The Archaeology of Human Bones**, London.
Oddy, W.A. (Ed) (1992)	**The Art of the Conservator**, London.
Prag, J. & Neave, R.	**Making Faces: using Forensic and Archaeological Evidence**, London.
Renfrew, C. & Bahn, P. (1991)	**Archaeology, Theory, Methods and Practice** 3rd ed, London.
Renfrew, C. (2000)	**Loot, Legitimacy and Ownership**, London.
Roberts, C. & Manchester, K. (1995)	**The Archaeology of Disease**, London.
Rooskams, S. (2001)	**Excavation**, Cambridge.
Scollar, I.	**Archaeological Prospecting and Remote Sensing**, London.
Stiebing, W.H. (1993)	**Uncovering the Past**, Oxford.
Taylor, C. (1974)	**Fieldwork in Medieval Archaeology**, London.
Trigger, B. (1989)	**A History of Archaeological Thought**, London.
Wass, S. (1992)	**The Amateur Archaeologist**, London
Watkinson, D. & Neal, V. (Eds) (1998)	**First Aid for Finds**, 3rd ed., Hertford.
Webster, G. (1974)	**Practical Archaeology**, 2nd ed., London.
Wilson, D.R. (2000)	**Air Photo Interpretation for Archaeologists**, London.

GREAT BOOKS FROM GREENLIGHT

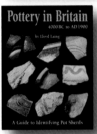
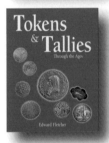
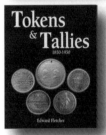

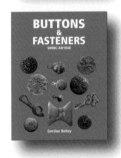

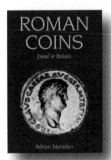

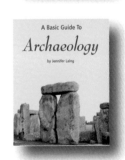